Library and Information Science

Library and Information Science

Shailendra Sengar

ANMOL PUBLICATIONS PVT. LTD.
NEW DELHI-110 002 (INDIA)

ANMOL PUBLICATIONS PVT. LTD.
H.O.: 4374/4B, Ansari Road, Darya Ganj,
New Delhi-110 002 (India)
Ph.: 23278000, 23261597

B.O.: No. 1015, Ist Main Road, BSK IIIrd Stage
IIIrd Phase, IIIrd Block
Bangalore - 560 085 (India)
Visit us at: www.anmolpublications.com

Library and Information Science

First Published, 2008

ISBN 978-81-261-3437-3

PRINTED IN INDIA

Printed at Mehra Offset Press, Delhi.

Contents

Contents

Preface

This Encyclopaedic Series of Career and Vocational Guidance Covers careers, describing jobs, places of employment, working conditions, qualifications, education and training. This has been developed to aid career and counsellors and job placement coordinators in planning activities for students and potential students about career vocational education programs. It contains a career and vocational guidance model which clarifies what career and vocational guidance services mean and what planners should include in their activities. The model shows an interrelatedness among major thrusts with career development being a central theme of vocational guidance. All of the thrusts depicted in the model represent essential services that should be available to students in career and vocational education programs. The encyclopaedia deals with various sections which correspond to the major thrusts identified in the model: (1) career development; (2) recruitment; (3) guidance and counselling; (4) placement; (5) follow-up and follow-through; and (6) consultation. Each section contains an outline of the perceived needs of the topic, an overview of the topic relative to career and vocational guidance, and some suggested activities and strategies that may be useful in meeting student needs.

It also contains current information about occupations, employment trends, and job searching. Materials on career decision-making, internships, and salaries are also located in each volume. This Series of Encyclopaedia helps students assess their potential for various careers.

Shailendra Sengar

1

Library and Information Science

Library Science

Library science, not to be confused with librarianship (non-science), is an interdisciplinary science incorporating the humanities, law and applied science to study topics related to libraries, the collection, organization and dissemination of information resources and the political economy of information. Historically, library science has also included Archival science. "The distinction between a library and an archive is relatively modern".

This includes how information resources are organized to serve the needs of select user groups, how people interact with classification systems and technology, how information is acquired, evaluated and applied by people in and outside of libraries as well as cross-culturally, how people are trained and educated for careers in libraries, the ethics that guide library service and organization, the legal status of libraries and information resources and the applied science of computer technology used in documentation and records management. Academic courses in library science typically include Collection management, Information Systems and Technology, Cataloging and classification, Reference, Statistics and Management.

Library science is constantly evolving, incorporating new topics like Database Management, Information Architecture and Knowledge Management, for example. There is no generally agreed distinction between library science, library and information science and librarianship. To a certain extent they can be considered equivalent terms, perhaps adopted to increase the "science" aspect, or improve the popular image of librarians.

The term library and information science (LIS) is sometimes used; most librarians consider it as only a terminological variation, intended to emphasize the scientific and technical foundations of the subject and its relationship with information science. LIS should not be confused with information theory, the mathematical study of the concept of information, or information science, a field related to computer science and cognitive science.

One operational view, implied by some of the textbooks, is that librarianship means the professional aspects of work as a librarian, such as certification, in-service training and issues of gender equality.

History

Library and information science, it may be argued, began with the first effort to organize a collection of information and provide access to that information.

Early History: At Ugarit in Syria excavations have revealed a palace library, temple library and two private libraries which date back to around 1200 BCE, containing diplomatic texts as well as poetry and other literary forms. In the 7th century, King Ashurbanipal of Assyria assembled what is considered "the first systematically collected library" at Nineveh; previous collections functioned more as passive archives. The legendary Library of Alexandria is perhaps the best known example of an early library, flourishing in the 3rd century BC and possibly inspired by Demetrius Phalereus.

Ancient Information Retrieval: One of the curators of the imperial library in the Han Dynasty is believed to have been the first to establish a library classification system and the first book notation system. At this time the library catalogue was written on scrolls of fine silk and stored in silk bags.

Jefferson's Method: Thomas Jefferson, whose library at Monticello consisted of thousands of books, devised a classification system inspired by the Baconian method which grouped books more or less by subject rather than alphabetically, as it was previously done. Jefferson's collection became the nucleus of our national collection when it was transferred to the United States Congress after a fire destroyed Congress' library during the War of 1812. The Jefferson collection was the start of what we now know as the Library of Congress.

20th Century: The term "library science" first appeared in the early 1930's, in the title of S. R. Ranganathan's The Five Laws of Library Science, published in 1931 and in the title of Lee Pierce Butler's 1933 book, An introduction to library science (University of Chicago Press). Butler's new approach advocated research using quantitative methods and ideas in the social sciences with the aim of using librarianship to address society's information needs. This research agenda went against the more procedure-based approach of "library economy," which was mostly confined to practical problems in the administration of libraries. While Ranganathan's approach was philosophical it was tied more to the day-to-day business of running a library.

In more recent years, with the growth of digital technology, the field has been greatly influenced by information science concepts. Although a basic understanding is critical to both library research and practical work, the area of information science has remained largely distinct both in training and in research interests.

Training in Librarianship

Most professional library jobs require a professional post-baccalaureate degree in library science, or one of its equivalent terms, library and information science as a basic credential. In the United States and Canada the certification usually comes from a Master's degree granted by an ALA -accredited institution, so even non-scholarly librarians have an originally academic background. In the United Kingdom, however, there have been moves to broaden the entry requirements to professional library posts, such that qualifications in, or experience of, a number of other disciplines have become more acceptable. For the main discussion of this topic, see Education for librarianship.

Subdisciplines: Subdisciplines of library science include the study of:

- Human Information Behaviours (information-seeking, search strategies and use)
- Knowledge Organization (which includes bibliographies, cataloging, classification, indexing & abstracting, metadata, semantic & syntactic analysis (controlled vocabularies, etc.))
- Digital libraries
- Collection development
- Public reference and other services
- Scholarly communication (includes bibliometrics, informetrics, scientometrics, webmetrics)

Types of library science professionals:

- Librarian
- Curator
- Archivist
- Computer, Data and Information Systems professionals
- Metadata Architects
- Cataloger
- Indexers
- Information broker
- Information architect
- Metadata Managers

Librarians in Different Types of Libraries

Public: The study of librarianship for public libraries covers issues such as cataloging, collection development for a diverse community, information literacy, community standards, public services-focused librarianship, serving a diverse community of adults, children and teens, Intellectual freedom, Censorship and legal and budgeting issues.

School: The study of school librarianship covers library services for children in schools up until (but not including) university. In some regions, the local government may have stricter standards for the education and certification of school librarians (who are often considered a special case of teacher), than for other librarians and the educational programme will include those local standards. School librarianship may also include issues of intellectual freedom; pedagogy; and how to build a cooperative curriculum with the teaching staff.

Academic: The study of academic librarianship covers library services for colleges and universities. Issues of special importance to the field may include copyright; technology, digital libraries and digital repositories; academic freedom; open access to scholarly works; as well as specialized knowledge of subject areas important to the institution and the relevant reference works. Some academic librarians are considered faculty and hold similar academic ranks as professors, while others are not. In either case, the minimal qualification is a Master's degree in Library Studies or Library Science and, in some cases, a Master's degree in another field.

Archives: The study of archives covers the training of archivists, librarians specially trained to maintain and build archives of records intended for historical preservation. Special issues include physical preservation of materials and mass deacidification; specialist catalogues; solo work; access; and appraisal. Many archivists are also trained historians specializing in the period covered by the archive.

Special: Special librarians include almost any other form of librarianship, including those who serve in medical libraries (and hospitals or medical schools), corporations, news agency libraries, or other special collections. The issues at these libraries will be specific to the industries they inhabit, but may include solo work; corporate financing; specialized collection development; and extensive self-promotion to potential patrons.

Preservation: Preservation librarians most often work in academic libraries. Their focus is on the management of preservation activities that seek to maintain access to content within books, manuscripts, archival materials and other library resources. Examples of activities managed by preservation librarians include binding, conservation, digital and analog reformatting, digital preservation and environmental monitoring.

Theory and Practice: Many practicing librarians do not contribute to LIS scholarship but focus on daily operations of their own library systems. Other practicing librarians, particularly in academic libraries, do perform original scholarly LIS research and contribute to the academic end of the field.

On this basis, it has sometimes been proposed that LIS is distinct from librarianship, in a way analogous to the difference between medicine and doctoring. In this view, librarianship, the application of library science, would comprise the practical services rendered by librarians in their day-to-day attempts to meet the needs of library patrons. Other uses of these terms do not make the distinction and treat them as synonyms. Powell's widely used introductory textbook does not make a formal distinction, but its bibliography uses the word librarianship as the heading for articles about the library profession.

Current Issues in LIS:

- Education for librarianship
- Information policy
- Information communication technologies (ICT's)
- Information Society
- Equity of Access
- Sustainability and ICT's
- Children's Internet Protection Act
- Censorship
- Information explosion
- Information literacy
- Government Information
- Decreased funding for established libraries
- Copyright
- Intellectual property rights
- Intellectual freedom
- Digital divide
- Open access
- Patriot Act

- Public lending right
- Slow fires
- Serials crisis
- Current digital/scanning technologies
- Remote access

Preservation (Library and Archival Science)

Preservation is a branch of Library and Information Science concerned with maintaining or restoring access to artifacts, documents and records through the study, diagnosis, treatment and prevention of decay and damage.

It should be distinguished from conservation which refers to the treatment and repair of individual items to slow decay or restore them to a usable state. Conservation is occasionally used interchangeably with preservation, particularly outside the professional literature.

History

Antecedents:

1. Oral tradition or oral culture, the transmission of information from one generation to the next without a writing system.
2. Antiquarian practices, including scribal practice, burial practice, the libraries at Pergamum, Alexandria and other ancient archives.
3. Medieval practices, including the scriptorium and relic collection
4. Renaissance and the changing conception of artists and works of art
5. Enlightenment and the Encyclopedists
6. Romantic movement's imperative to preserve

Significant events:

- 1933: William Barrow introduces the field of conservation to paper deacidification when he publishes a paper on the acid paper problem. In later studies, Barrow tested paper from American books made between 1900 and 1949 and learned that after forty years the books had lost on average

96 percent of their original strength; after less than ten years, they had already lost 64 percent. Barrow determined that this rapid deterioration was not the direct result of using wood-pulp fibres, since rag papers of this period were also aging rapidly, but rather due to the residual sulfuric acid produced in both rag and wood pulp papers. Manufacturing methods used after 1870 employed sulfuric acid for sizing and bleaching the paper. Earlier papermaking methods left the final product only mildly alkaline or even neutral. Such paper has maintained its strength for 300 to 800 years, despite sulphur dioxide and other air pollutants. (2. The Library, Edited by Rolland E. Stevens) Barrow's 1933 article on the fragile state of wood pulp paper predicted the shelf life of this paper was approximately 40-50 years. At that point the paper would begin to show signs of deterioration and he concluded that research for a new media on which to write and print was needed.

- 1966: The Flood of the River Arno in Florence, Italy damaged or destroyed millions of rare books and lead to the development of restoration laboratories and new methods in conservation. This event awakened many historians, librarians and other professionals to the importance of having a preservation plan. Many consider this flood to be one of the worst disasters since the burning of the Alexandria Library in ancient Rome. It spurred a resurgence in the profession of preservation and conservation worldwide.
- 1987: Terry Saunders releases the film Slow Fires: On the Preservation of the Human Record which examines paper embrittlement resulting from acid decay

Significant preservationists

- William Barrow (1904-1967) was an American chemist and paper conservator and a pioneer of library and archives conservation. He introduced the field of conservation to paper deacidification through alkalization.
- Paul N. Banks (1934 - 2000) was Conservator and Head of the Conservation Department at the Newberry Library

from 1964 to 1981 and published regularly on bookbinding, book and paper conservation and problems related to conservation. He designed and implemented a curriculum for Columbia University's School of Library Science that dealt directly with preservation training.

- Pamela Darling, author and historian, was Preservation Specialist for the Association of Research Libraries. Her works include materials to aid libraries in establishing their own comprehensive preservation programmes.
- Carolyn Harris worked as head of Columbia University Libraries' Preservation Division from 1981 until 1987, where she worked closely with Paul Banks. She published extensive research throughout her career, especially dealing with mass deacidification of wood-pulp paper.
- Peter Waters delved into the areas of disaster preparedness and the salvage of water-damaged paper goods. His published works outline procedures such as freezing followed by vacuum freeze drying to rescue wet books.
- Nicholson Baker is a contemporary American novelist and author of Double Fold, a criticism of libraries' destruction of paper-based media.

The Paul Banks and Carolyn Harris Preservation Award for outstanding preservation specialists in library and archival science, is given annually by the Association for Library Collections & Technical Services, a subdivision of the American Library Association. It is awarded in recognition of professional preservation specialists who have made significant contributions to the field, Banks/Harris award winners:

- Sarah Buchanan 2001 - Buchanan received the award in recognition of years of service in the preservation field while an associate professor at the University of Pittsburgh School of Information Science
- Ellen McCrady 2002-Since 1975, McCrady has edited and published the "Abbey Newsletter", covering important information for preservation professionals. She also conducts research regarding papermaking and acid testing.

- John F. Dean 2003 - Since its inception in 1985, Dean has led the Department of Preservation and Conservation at Cornell University.
- Jan Merrill-Oldham 2004-As the Malloy-Rabinowitz Preservation Librarian at Harvard University, Merrill-Oldham oversees the Weissman Preservation Centre and the Preservation and Imaging Department.
- Paul Conway 2005 - Conway has worked with Yale, [Duke University, Duke] and the University of Michigan after beginning his career at the Gerald R. Ford Presidential Library. His research and educational work focuses primarily on digital preservation and electronic media.
- Gary Frost 2006-Currently a conservator at the University of Iowa Libraries, Frost has been an educator and practicioner in the field of library preservation for over 35 years.

Practices: Care and handling:

1. Exhibitions
2. Circulating collections
3. Special collections

Research and Testing: With old media deteriorating or showing their vulnerabilities and new media becoming available, research remains active in the field of conservation and preservation. Everything from how to preserve paper media to creating and maintaining electronic resources is being explored by students and professionals in library and information science. The two main issues that most libraries tend to face are the rapid disintegration of acidic paper and water damage (due to flooding, plumbing problems, etc.). Therefore, these areas of preservation, as well as new digital technologies, receive much of the research attention.

The American Library Association has many scholarly journals that publish articles on preservation topics, such as College and Research Libraries, Information Technology and Libraries and Library Resources and Technical Services. Scholarly periodicals in this field from other publishers include International Preservation News, Journal of the American

Institute for Conservation and Collection Management among many others.

Regional centres:

- The Conservation Center for Art and Historic Artifacts in Phildelphia, PA is a non-profit conservation laboratory specializing in the treatment of art and historic artifacts on paper. The Center also trains museum and library professionals in disaster planning, records and archives management.
- Northeast Document Conservation Center. Since its inception in 1973, the Center has instructed institutions and organizations, as well as librarians, conservators, preservationists and museum professionals in preservation care and procedures.

Vendor Services: Because of the complicated and often expensive nature of preservation activities, libraries, museums and other educational facilities are often unable to adequately repair and preserve their own items. Many private entities have stepped in to provide preservation and repair services. Listed here are many of these businesses.

Archives and Special Collections:

- Archivart
- Carr McLean
- Conservation Resources
- Demco
- Gaylord
- Light Impressions
- Hollinger Corp.
- Metal Edge
- Paige Company
- Talas
- University Products

Library Binding: One method of preserving a library collection is to rebind paperback items in hard cover library binding. Some facilities do this themselves, but there are also commercial companies that work exclusively in library binding.

- The HF Group
- ICI Binding Corporation
- Bridgeport Library Binding Services
- Ocker & Trapp Library Binding, Inc.
- Acme Bookbinding

Exhibitions:

- Benchmark

Branches

Functional areas:

- Collections Care refers to the general maintenance and preventive care of a collection as a whole. This can include activities such as security, environmental monitoring, preservation surveys and more specialized activities such as mass deacidification.
- Conservation refers to the treatment and repair of individual items to slow decay or restore them to a usable state. Conservation is occasionally used interchangeably with preservation, particularly outside the professional literature.
- Digital preservation refers to the maintenance of digitally stored information. This should not be confused with digitization, which is a process of creating digital information which must, in turn, be digitally preserved. Means of digital preservation include refreshing, migration, replication and emulation.
- Disaster Preparedness refers to the practice of arranging for the necessary resources and planning the best course of action to prevent or minimize damage to a collection in the event of a disaster of any level of magnatude.
- Reformatting refers to the practice of creating copies of an object in another type of data storage device. Reformatting processes include microfilming and digitization.

Media specific:

- Paper
    - o Acid-free paper

- Books
- Visual materials
    - o Colour photography
    - o Architectural reprography, a variety of technologies and media used to make multiple copies of original drawings or records created by architects, engineers, map-makers and related professionals.
- Recorded sound
    - o Magnetic audiotape
- Oral history preservation
- Moving image .
    - o Moving Image Preservation Education .

Education: One of the biggest challenges in the field of preservation today is educating a library's community, especially librarians and other staff, in the best ways to handle materials as well as the conditions in which particular materials will decay the least. This challenge is exacerbated by the fact that preservation is a peripheral element of most library science curricula; indeed, there are few places where one can receive a specialized education in preservation.

The primary degree granting institution for library and archival preservation is the University of Texas at Austin's School of Information Science. The conservation and preservation programme is offered in partnership with the Kilgarlin Center for Preservation of the Cultural Record and trains both conservators and preservation administrators. Other conservation programmes in the United States focus on Art Conservation and are considered to be more museum focused than library focused. These programmes are all part of the Association of North American Graduate Programmes in the Conservation of Cultural Property (ANAGPIC).

The Rutgers Preservation Management Institute (PMI) provides postgraduate training in preservation administration for working librarians who have already completed a Master's degree. UT Austin also offers certificates of advanced study in conservation and preservation to librarians who already hold their MLS.

Another educational resource available to preservationists is the Northeast Document Conservation Center or NEDCC. This institution was founded in 1973 as a reaction to the growing problem of paper deterioration occurring in repositories in the New England area. The Center provides institutions and organizations, as well as librarians, conservators, preservationists and museum professionals, with help in learning proper care and procedures to better preserve the integrity of their collections.

The institution provides a variety of services such as imaging, surveys and consultations and digitation. They also assist with disaster planning. The educational opportunities it provides include provision of workshops, conferences and specialized trainings. Additional online courses are also available. For instance, some of the workshops offered by the NEDCC include: Basic Preservation, Collections Care, Emergency Preparedness, Integrated Pest Management (IPM), Identification and Care of Photographs, Basic and Intermediate Book Repair, Basic Paper Repair, Preservation of Scrapbooks, Preservation Technologies, Holdings Maintenance, Creating and Maintaining Digital Collections, Scanning Training and Grant Writing.

Additional preservation education is available to librarians through various professional organizations, such as:

- American Institute for Conservation of Historic and Artistic Works, AIC
- American Library Association (ALA)
- Amigoes Library Services Preservation Service
- Association for Information and Image Management (AIIM)
- Association for Recorded Sound Collections (ARSC)
- Buffalo State College. Art Conservation Department, Buffalo, NY
- Campbell Center for Historic Preservation Studies, Mount Carroll, IL.
- George Eastman House. School of Film & Video Preservation Rochester, NY

- The Kilgarlin Center for Preservation of the Cultural Record
- Library Binding Institute
- New York University. Conservation Center, Institute of Fine Arts, New York, NY
- North Bennet Street School. Boston, MA
- Northeast Document Conservation Center (NEDCC)
- The Conservation Center for Art and Historic Artifacts in Phildelphia, PA (link below)
- Queen's University. Master of Art Conservation Programme, Ont, Canada
- Rare Book School (RBS) at the University of Virginia
- Society of American Archivists
- Southeastern Library Network (SOLINET)
- University of Delaware. Winterthur Art Conservation Programme, Newark, DE
- The National Archives.

Non-Academic Facilities and Preservation: Public Libraries: Limited, tax-driven funding can often interfere with the ability for public libaries to engage in extensive preservation activities. Materials, particularly books, are often much easier to replace than to repair when damaged or worn. Public libraries usually try to tailor their services to meet the needs and desires of their local communities, which could cause an emphasis on aquiring new materials over preserving old ones. Librarians working in public facilities frequently have to make complicated decisions about how to best serve their patrons. Commonly, public library systems work with each other and sometimes with more academic libraries through interlibrary loan programmes. By sharing resources, they are able to expand upon what might be available to their own patrons and share the burdens of preservation across a greater array of systems.

Archival Repositories and Special Collections: Archival facilities focus specifically on rare and fragile materials. With staff trained in appropriate techniques, archives are often available to many public and private library facilities as an alternative to destroying older materials. Items that are unique, such as photographs, or items that are out of print, can be preserved in archival facilities more easily than in many library settings.

Museums: Because so many museum holdings are unique, including print materials, art and other objects, preservationists are often most active in this setting.

Legal Issues: Reformatting, or in any other way copying an item's contents, raises obvious copyright issues. In many cases, a library is allowed to make a limited number of copies of an item for preservation purposes.

Criticism: There is a longstanding tension between preservation of and access to library materials, particularly in the area of special collections. Handling materials promotes their progression to an unusable state, especially if they are handled carelessly. On the other hand, materials must be used in order to gain any benefit from them. In a collection with valuable materials, this conflict is often resolved by a number of measures which can include heightened security, requiring the use of gloves for photographs, restricting the materials researchers may bring with them into a reading room and restricting use of materials to patrons who are not able satisfy their research needs with less valuable copies of an item. These measures can seem intimidating to less experienced researchers who might feel that these preservation measures are in place solely to keep materials out of the hands of the public.

There is also controversy surrounding preservation methods. Often after items have been digitized or reformatted onto other media such as microfilm, the originals are destroyed. This sometimes proves to be problematic when the new media itself begins to deteriorate, if the new copies are of poor quality, or if they are incompletely copied. Many digitized items, such as back issues of periodicals, are provided by publishers and databases on a subscription basis. If these companies were for any number of reasons cease providing access to their digital information, facilities that elected to discard paper copies of these periodicals will no longer be able to use such items. Discussion as to the best ways to utilize digital technologies is therefore ongoing and the practice continues to evolve.

Library and Information Science

Library and information science (LIS) is the study of issues related to libraries. This includes academic studies (most often surveys) about how library resources are used and how people interact with library systems. These studies tend to be specific to certâin libraries at certain times. The organization of knowledge for efficient retrieval of relevant information is also a major research goal of LIS. Basic topics in library science include the acquisition, classification and preservation of library materials. In a more present-day view, a fervent outgrowth of LIS is information architecture. LIS should not be confused with information theory, the mathematical study of the concept of information.

Library science is distinct from librarianship, which is the practical services rendered by librarians in their day-to-day attempt to meet the needs of library patrons. Librarianship tends not to create new knowledge, nor to strive to advance any field or discipline. Librarians only rarely engage in library science and then usually outside their jobs as librarians. But the study of library science is part of the requisite training of librarians. "Information" and "documentation" means non-book materials that university libraries deal with, such as magazines, scientific journals, technical reports and access to online databases.

The term library and information science should not be broken into these separate pieces. Library and Information Science is a hybrid academic field that grew from library schools' fight for survival in the electronic age. The politics of academia, issues of status and prestige, issues of perceived obsolescence and other forces created these programmes. Programmes in library and information science are interdisciplinary, overlapping with the fields of systems' analysis, computer science, statistics and various parts of the social sciences.

The field of library and information science is not defined by its output of information specialists, but by the "information specialists" who remain in academia teaching and doing research, by its literature, its journals and all the other ways in which an academic discipline is defined, the study of which, by the way, falls within the scope of Library and Information Science.

Important LIS institutions and resources:

- The National Information Standards Organization
- Indiana University SLIS.
- Syracuse University School of Information Studies.
- University of Michigan School of Information.
- University of Pittsburgh School of Information Sciences.
- University of California Berkeley School of Information Management & Systems.
- University of Washington Information School.
- University of North Carolina at Chapel Hill School of Information and Library Science.
- University of North Texas School of Library and Information Sciences.
- Dominican University (River Forest, IL).
- University of Illinois Graduate School of Library and Information Science.
- University of Rhode Island Graduate School of Library and Information Studies.
- Simmons College Graduate School of Library & Information Science.
- OCLC (Online Computer Library Center).
- American Library Association.
- Canadian Library Association.
- Australian Library and Information Association.
- American Society for Information Science and Technology.
- International Federation of Library Associations and Institutions (IFLA).

Some current LIS issues:

- childhood internet protection act
- information explosion
- information retrieval
- Library Instruction

- knowledge management
- reference sources
- information storage
- information literacy
- slow fires
- mass deacidification
- information architecture
- public lending right
- Patriot Act

Library Management: Basic tasks in library management include:

- planning the acquistion of materials
- classification of materials
- preservation of materials (especially rare and fragile materials such as manuscripts)
- borrowing materials
- developing and administering library computer systems

More long-term issues include the planning of the construction of new libraries or extensions to existing ones.

The School of Information Studies prepares students for careers in library and information professions. The School provides students with the opportunity to develop attitudes associated with progressive information services and to develop an understanding of the value, role and application of modern technology as it relates to library operations and the transfer of information. The School's graduate programme is fully accredited by the American Library Association.

In harmony with the mission of the University of Wisconsin-Milwaukee, a major urban research institute, the School of Information Studies strives to make significant contributions towards extending and enhancing the quality of information services and the promotion of information and technological literacy to a diverse society. The School of Information Studies is committed to excellence in instruction, research and service. Goals of the school are:

1. To prepare professionals who are able to provide leadership and adapt to change in a technological and knowledge-based environment for careers in libraries, school media centres, information systems and related areas, according to accepted professional standards.
2. To enrich the library and information science profession through recruitment of students with strong academic skills from diverse cultural, geographic and subject backgrounds.
3. To enable undergraduate students to achieve qualifications to pursue careers in the information professions through the provision of degree and certificate programmes.
4. To enable students to develop specializations in the information professions at the graduate level through the provision of single and dual degree programmes.
5. To promote a research orientation through participation in the Doctor of Philosophy degree programme.
6. To contribute to the international knowledge base of library and information science through research and publication.
7. To facilitate the development, provision and evaluation of library and information services through consultation services to individual organizations and leadership in professional associations locally, statewide, nationally and internationally.
8. To offer opportunities for professionals and the wider community to update their skills and knowledge through advanced and continuing education courses, workshops and programmes offered nationally and internationally.

The purpose of the MLIS programme is to prepare librarians and information professionals who are able to manage change in an urbanized, technologically oriented and knowledge-based society. The MLIS programme provides a systematic course of study which enables individuals with a strong service orientation to apply principles of library and information science, use current methods and tools and recognize the value of research.

Students may elect to specialize according to the type of library or information service which best meets their needs: *i.e.*, school, public, academic, or special; or to follow a more generalized approach.

Graduates of the Master of Library and Information Science degree programme are expected to demonstrate the following competencies:

1. To apply scientific principles in developing and managing information resources designed to meet user needs and interests.
2. To analyze, describe and organize resources for effective and efficient retrieval and dissemination of information.
3. To utilize knowledge of information sources, services and systems to meet the informational needs of users.
4. To apply management principles in planning, developing, marketing and evaluating library and information services.
5. To work in specialized areas of library and information service, utilizing knowledge obtained from concentrations within the School and in other disciplines.
6. To build upon current knowledge of information and communication theories and technologies in planning, design, development and delivery of information services.

The master's degree programme is designed to support each of these objectives with appropriate coursework and educational experiences. The School of Information Studies in collaboration with the School of Education offers post-bachelor's programmes leading to State of Wisconsin licensing as Initial Instructional Library Media Specialist, Instructional Library Media Specialist and Instructional Library Media Supervisor.

Students admitted to the Master of Library and Information Science degree programme can incorporate in their degree programme the courses for these licenses to the extent that these courses satisfy the degree requirements, either as required core courses or as electives. Licenses will be granted only to those persons who are eligible to hold a Wisconsin license to teach in the elementary or secondary schools or who have completed an approved elementary or secondary classroom teacher preparation programme. For additional information about these licenses and their relationship to the master's degree, consult the School Library Media Coordinator.

The advanced courses offered by the School of Information Studies may be elected on a non-degree basis by postmaster's students who wish to continue their professional education or special competence in some phase of urban library and information services. See section below titled the "Certificate of Advanced Study in Library and Information Science" for a formal programme of postmaster's education. The School's graduate courses are also open to graduate students in other fields of study, provided that they have completed the appropriate basic courses (or their equivalent).

Coordinated Degree Programmes: In cooperation with the Department of Music in the Peck School of the Arts and the Departments of Anthropology, English, Geography and History, the Urban Studies programme and the Foreign Language and Literature programme in the College of Letters and Science, the School of Information Studies offers the following coordinated degree programmes:

MM/MLIS. Master of Music/Master of Library and Information Studies programme to prepare students for positions as music librarians. Students in the MM degree programme will pursue a concentration in Music History and Literature, 54 credits.

MA/MLIS. A Master of Arts in Geography/Master of Library and Information Science programme to prepare students for positions as map librarians, 48 credits.

MA/MLIS. A Master of Arts in History/Master of Library and Information Science programme to prepare students for positions as archivists, 48 credits.

MS/MLIS. A Master of Science in Urban Studies/Master of Library and Information Science programme to prepare students for positions as urban information specialists, 54 credits.

MAFLL/MLIS. A Master of Arts in Foreign Language and Literature/Master of Library and Information Science programme to prepare students for positions as librarians in a variety of libraries and curators of special subject collections, 51 credits.

MA/MLIS. A Master of Arts in English/Master of Library and Information Science programme to prepare students for positions as humanities librarians and curators of special subject collections in the humanities, 51 credits.

MS/MLIS. A Master of Science in Anthropology/Master of Library and Information Science to prepare students for positions as curators of museum libraries and as information specialists and researchers for local history collections and state historical societies, 51 credits.

Prerequisite to the award of either degree in these coordinated programmes is the simultaneous award of its counterpart degree. For additional information on these programmes, see the Music, Geography, History, Urban Studies, Foreign Language and Literature, English and Anthropology sections of this Bulletin. Under the auspices of the doctoral programme in Urban Education, the School of Information Studies provides doctoral training with a specialization in Educational and Media Technology. Prospective doctoral students wishing to specialize in Educational and Media Technology must first be admitted to the Urban Education Doctoral Programme. Admission and general programme requirements can be obtained from the Director of Doctoral Studies in Urban Education. This specialization is described in detail in the Urban Education section of this Bulletin.

Librarians

Significant Points: A master's degree in library science usually is required; special librarians may need an additional graduate or professional degree.

A large number of retirements in the next decade is expected to result in many job openings for librarians to replace those who leave.

Librarians increasingly use information technology to perform research, classify materials and help students and library patrons seek information.

Nature of the Work: The traditional concept of a library is being redefined from a place to access paper records or books to one that also houses the most advanced media, including CD-ROM, the Internet, virtual libraries and remote access to a wide range of resources. Consequently, librarians, or information professionals, increasingly are combining traditional duties with tasks involving quickly changing technology. Librarians assist people in finding information and using it effectively for personal and professional purposes. Librarians must have knowledge of a wide variety of scholarly and public information sources and must follow trends related to publishing, computers and the media in order to oversee the selection and organization of library materials. Librarians manage staff and develop and direct information programmes and systems for the public, to ensure that information is organized in a manner that meets users' needs.

Most librarian positions incorporate three aspects of library work: User services, technical services and administrative services. Still, even librarians specializing in one of these areas have other responsibilities. Librarians in user services, such as reference and children's librarians, work with patrons to help them find the information they need.

The job involves analyzing users' needs to determine what information is appropriate, as well as searching for, acquiring and providing the information. The job also includes an instructional role, such as showing users how to access information. For example, librarians commonly help users navigate the Internet so they can search for relevant information efficiently. Librarians in technical services, such as acquisitions and cataloguing, acquire and prepare materials for use and often do not deal directly with the public. Librarians in administrative services oversee the management and planning of libraries: negotiate contracts for services, materials and equipment; supervise library employees; perform public-relations and fundraising duties; prepare budgets; and direct activities to ensure that everything functions properly.

In small libraries or information centres, librarians usually handle all aspects of the work. They read book reviews, publishers' announcements and catalogues to keep up with current literature and other available resources and they select and purchase materials from publishers, wholesalers and distributors. Librarians prepare new materials by classifying them by subject matter and describe books and other library materials to make them easy to find. Librarians supervise assistants, who prepare cards, computer records, or other access tools that direct users to resources. In large libraries, librarians often specialize in a single area, such as acquisitions, cataloguing, bibliography, reference, special collections, or administration. Teamwork is increasingly important to ensure quality service to the public.

Librarians also compile lists of books, periodicals, articles and audiovisual materials on particular subjects; analyze collections; and recommend materials. They collect and organize books, pamphlets, manuscripts and other materials in a specific field, such as rare books, genealogy, or music. In addition, they coordinate programmes such as storytelling for children and literacy skills and book talks for adults, conduct classes, publicize services, provide reference help, write grants and oversee other administrative matters. Librarians are classified according to the type of library in which they work: A public library; school library media center; college, university, or other academic library; or special library. Some librarians work with specific groups, such as children, young adults, adults, or the disadvantaged. In school library media centres, librarians-often called school media specialists-help teachers develop curricula, acquire materials for classroom instruction and sometimes team teach.

Librarians also work in information centres or libraries maintained by government agencies, corporations, law firms, advertising agencies, museums, professional associations, unions, medical centres, hospitals, religious organizations and research laboratories. They acquire and arrange an organization's information resources, which usually are limited to subjects of special interest to the organization. These special librarians can provide vital information services by preparing abstracts and indexes of current periodicals, organizing bibliographies, or analyzing background information and preparing reports on areas of particular interest. For example, a special librarian working for a corporation could provide the sales department with information on competitors or new developments affecting the field. A medical librarian may provide information about new medical treatments, clinical trials and standard procedures to health professionals, patients, consumers and corporations. Government document librarians, who work for government agencies and depository libraries in each of the States, preserve government publications, records and other documents that make up a historical record of government actions.

Many libraries have access to remote databases and maintain their own computerized databases. The widespread use of automation in libraries makes database-searching skills important to librarians. Librarians develop and index databases and help train users to develop searching skills for the information they need. Some libraries are forming consortiums with other libraries to allow patrons to access a wider range of databases and to submit information requests to several libraries simultaneously. The Internet also has greatly expanded the amount of available reference information. Librarians must be aware of how to use these resources in order to locate information.

Librarians with computer and information systems skills can work as automated-systems librarians, planning and operating computer systems and as information architects, designing information storage and retrieval systems and developing procedures for collecting, organizing, interpreting and classifying information. These librarians analyze and plan for future information needs. The increasing use of automated information systems is enabling librarians to focus on administrative and budgeting responsibilities, grant writing and specialized research requests, while delegating more technical and user services responsibilities to technicians.

More and more, librarians are applying their information management and research skills to arenas outside of libraries-for example, database development, reference tool development, information systems, publishing, Internet coordination, marketing, web content management and design and training of database users. Entrepreneurial librarians sometimes start their own consulting practices, acting as freelance librarians or information brokers and providing services to other libraries, businesses, or government agencies.

Working Conditions: Librarians spend a significant portion of time at their desks or in front of computer terminals; extended work at video display terminals can cause eyestrain and headaches. Assisting users in obtaining information or books for their jobs, homework, or recreational reading can be challenging and satisfying, but working with users under deadlines can be demanding and stressful. Some librarians lift and carry books and some climb ladders to reach high stacks, although most modern libraries have readily accessible stacks. Librarians in small organizations sometimes shelve books themselves.

More than 2 out of 10 librarians work part time. Public and college librarians often work weekends and evenings, as well as some holidays. School librarians usually have the same workday and vacation schedules as classroom teachers. Special librarians usually work normal business hours, but in fast-paced industries-such as advertising or legal services-they can work longer hours when needed.

Training, Other Qualifications and Advancement: A master's degree in library science (MLS) is necessary for librarian positions in most public, academic and special libraries and in some school libraries. The Federal Government requires that the librarians it employs have an MLS or the equivalent in education and experience. Many colleges and universities offer MLS programmes, but employers often prefer graduates of the approximately 56 schools accredited by the American Library Association. Most MLS programmes require a bachelor's degree, but no specific undergraduate programme is required.

Most MLS programmes take one year to complete; some take two. A typical graduate programme includes courses in the foundations of library and information science, including the history of books and printing, intellectual freedom and censorship and the role of libraries and information in society. Other basic courses cover the selection and processing of materials, the organization of information, reference tools and strategies and user services. Courses are adapted to educate librarians to use new resources brought about by advancing technology, such as online reference systems, Internet search methods and automated circulation systems. Course options can include resources for children or young adults; classification, cataloguing, indexing and abstracting; library administration; and library automation. Computer-related course work is an increasingly important part of an MLS degree. Some programmes offer interdisciplinary degrees combining technical courses in information science with traditional training in library science.

The MLS degree provides general preparation for library work, but some individuals specialize in a particular area, such as reference, technical services, or children's services. A Ph.D. degree in library and information science is advantageous for a college teaching position or for a top administrative job in a college or university library or large library system.

In addition to an MLS degree, most special librarians supplement their education with knowledge of the field in which they are specializing, sometimes earning a master's, doctoral, or professional degree in the subject. Areas of specialization include medicine, law, business, engineering and the natural and social sciences. For example, a librarian working for a law firm may also be a licensed attorney, holding both library science and law degrees, while medical librarians should have a strong background in the sciences. In some jobs, knowledge of a foreign language is needed.

States generally have certification requirements for librarians in public schools and local libraries, though there are wide variations among States. Many require school librarians, often called library media specialists, to be certified as teachers in addition to having courses in library science. An MLS is needed in some States, often with a library media specialization, while in others a master's in education with a specialty in school library media or educational media is needed. Twenty-four States also require certification of librarians employed in local library systems, while several others have voluntary certification guidelines.

Librarians participate in continuing education and training, once they are on the job, in order to keep abreast of new information systems brought about by changing technology. Experienced librarians can advance to administrative positions, such as department head, library director, or chief information officer.

Employment: Librarians held about 159,000 jobs in 2004. Most worked in school and academic libraries, but one-fourth worked in public libraries. The remainder worked in special libraries or as information professionals for companies and other organizations.

Job Outlook: Employment of librarians is expected to grow more slowly than the average for all occupations over the 2004-14 period. However, job opportunities are expected to be very good because a large number of librarians are expected to retire in the coming decade. More than 3 in 5 librarians are aged 45 or older and will become eligible for retirement in the next 10 years, which will result in many job openings. Also, the number of people going into this profession has fallen in recent years, resulting in more jobs than applicants in some cases.

Growth in the number of librarians will be limited by government budget constraints and the increasing use of computerized information storage and retrieval systems. Both will result in the hiring of fewer librarians and the replacement of librarians with less costly library technicians and assistants. Computerized systems make cataloguing easier, allowing library technicians to perform the work.

In addition, many libraries are equipped for users to access library computers directly from their homes or offices. That way, users can bypass librarians altogether and conduct research on their own. However, librarians will still be needed to manage staff, help users develop database-searching techniques, address complicated reference requests and define users' needs.

Jobs for librarians outside traditional settings will grow the fastest over the decade. Nontraditional librarian jobs include working as information brokers and working for private corporations, non-profit organizations and consulting firms. Many companies are turning to librarians because of their research and organizational skills and their knowledge of computer databases and library automation systems. Librarians can review vast amounts of information and analyze, evaluate and organize it according to a company's specific needs. Librarians also are hired by organizations to set up information on the Internet. Librarians working in these settings may be classified as systems analysts, database specialists and trainers, webmasters or web developers, or local area network (LAN) coordinators.

Earnings: Salaries of librarians vary according to the individual's qualifications and the type, size and location of the library. Librarians with primarily administrative duties often have greater earnings. Median annual earnings of librarians in May 2004 were $45,900. The middle 50 percent earned between $36,980 and $56,960. The lowest 10 percent earned less than $28,930 and the highest 10 percent earned more than $70,200. Median annual earnings in the industries employing the largest numbers of librarians in May 2004 were as follows:

Colleges, universities and professional schools	$47,830
Elementary and secondary schools	47,580
Local government	42,500
Other information services	40,000

The average annual salary for all librarians in the Federal Government in non-supervisory, supervisory and managerial positions was $74,630 in 2005.

About three in ten librarians are a member of a union or are covered under a union contract.

Related Occupations: Librarians play an important role in the transfer of knowledge and ideas by providing people with access to the information they need and want. Jobs requiring similar analytical, organizational and communication skills include archivists, curators and museum technicians; and computer and information scientists, research. School librarians have many duties similar to those of school teachers. Librarians are increasingly storing, cataloguing and accessing information with computers. Other jobs that use similar computer skills include computer systems analysts and computer scientists and database administrators.

2

Study and Programme

Library Assistants, Clerical

Significant Points: Minimal training requirements and flexible schedules make this occupation appealing to students, retirees and others interested in part-time work. Most libraries use electronic cataloging systems so computers skills are essential.

Nature of the Work: Library assistants, clerical—sometimes referred to as *library media assistants*, *library aides*, or *circulation assistants*—assist librarians and library technicians in organizing library resources and making them available to users. (Librarians and library technicians are discussed elsewhere in the *Handbook*.) Library assistants register patrons so that they can borrow materials from the library and then issue a library card.

At the circulation desk, library assistants lend and collect books, periodicals, video-tapes and other materials. When an item is borrowed, assistants scan the patron's library card and the material to record the transaction in the library database; they then print a receipt with the due date or stamp the due date on the item. When an item is returned, assistants inspect returned materials for damage and enter the materials into the circulation database. Electronic circulation systems are able to automatically generate overdue notices reminding patrons that their materials are overdue, but library assistants review the record for accuracy before sending out the notice. They also answer patrons' questions and refer those they cannot answer to a librarian.

Throughout the library, assistants sort returned books, periodicals and other items and put them on their designated shelves, in the appropriate files, or in storage areas. They locate materials to be lent, to either a patron or another library. Because nearly all card catalogues are computerized, library assistants must be familiar with computers. Before reshelving returned materials, if they notice any damage, these workers try to repair it. For example, they may use tape or paste to repair torn pages or book covers and use other specialized processes to repair more valuable materials.

Some library assistants specialize in helping patrons who have vision problems. Sometimes referred to as *library, talking-books*, or *braille-and-talking-books clerks*, they review the borrower's list of desired reading materials. They locate those materials or closely related substitutes from the library collection of large-type or braille volumes, tape cassettes and open-reel talking books; complete the requisite paperwork; and give or mail the materials to the borrower.

Working Conditions: Library assistants who prepare library materials may sit at desks or computer terminals for long periods and can develop headaches or eyestrain from working with the terminals. Some duties can be repetitive and boring, such as shelving new or returned materials. Others can be rewarding, such as assisting patrons who are performing computer searches with the use of local and regional library networks and cooperatives. Library assistants may lift and carry books, climb ladders to reach high stacks and bend low to shelve books on bottom shelves.

Library assistants in school libraries work regular school hours. Those in public libraries and college and university (academic) libraries also work weekends, evenings and some holidays. About half of all library assistants work part time, making the job appealing to retirees, students and others interested in flexible schedules.

Training, Other Qualifications and Advancement: Training requirements for library assistants are generally minimal; most libraries prefer to hire workers with a high school diploma or GED, but little to no formal post-secondary training is expected. Some employers hire individuals with experience in other clerical jobs, while others train inexperienced workers on the job. Given the rapid spread of automation in libraries, computer skills are needed for most jobs; knowledge of databases and other library automation systems is especially useful.

Library assistants usually advance by assuming added responsibilities. Many begin by performing simple jobs such as shelving books or cataloging new books and periodicals when they arrive. After gaining experience, they may move into positions that allow them to interact with patrons, such as manning the circulation desk. Experienced aids may be able to advance into library technician positions, which involve more responsibility in providing library services to patrons.

Employment: Library assistants held about 109,000 jobs in 2004. More than half of these workers were employed by local governments in public libraries; most of the remaining employees worked in school, college and university libraries. Opportunities for flexible schedules are abundant; nearly half of these workers were on part-time schedules.

Job Outlook: Employment of library assistants is expected to grow as fast as the average for all occupations through 2014. Efforts to contain costs in local governments and academic institutions of all types may result in more hiring of library support staff than librarians. Also, due to changing roles within libraries, library assistants are taking on more responsibility.

Many library assistants leave this relatively low-paying occupation for other jobs that offer higher pay or full-time work, so job opportunities should be good for persons interested in jobs as library assistants.

The work is often attractive to retirees, students and others who want a part-time schedule and there is a lot of movement into and out of the occupation. Some positions become available as library assistants move within the organization. Library assistants can be promoted to library technicians and, eventually, supervisory positions in public-service or technical-service areas. Advancement opportunities are greater in large libraries.

Because most are employed by public institutions, library assistants are not directly affected by the ups and downs of the business cycle. However, some of these workers may lose their jobs if there are cuts in government budgets.

Earnings: Median hourly earnings of library assistants, clerical were $9.96 in May 2004. The middle 50 percent earned between $7.77 and $12.89. The lowest 10 percent earned less than $6.41 and the highest 10 percent earned more than $16.08.

Office and Administrative Support Worker

Significant Points: Most jobs are filled by promoting office or administrative support workers from within the organization.

Office automation will cause employment in some office and administrative support occupations to grow slowly or even decline, resulting in slower-than-average growth among supervisors and managers.

Applicants are likely to encounter keen competition because their numbers should greatly exceed the number of job openings.

Nature of the Work: All organizations need timely and effective office and administrative support to operate efficiently. Office and administrative support supervisors and managers coordinate this support. These workers are employed in virtually every sector of the economy, working in positions as varied as teller supervisor, customer services manager, or shipping and receiving supervisor.

Although specific functions of office and administrative support supervisors and managers vary significantly, they share many common duties. For example, supervisors perform administrative tasks to ensure that their staffs can work efficiently. Equipment and machinery used in their departments must be in good working order. If the computer system goes down or a fax machine malfunctions, the supervisors must try to correct the problem or alert repair personnel. They also request new equipment or supplies for their department when necessary.

Planning the work and supervising the staff are key functions of this job. To do these effectively, the supervisor must know the strengths and weaknesses of each member of the staff, as well as the results required from and time allotted to each job. Supervisors must make allowances for unexpected staff absences and other disruptions by adjusting assignments or performing the work themselves if the situation requires it.

After allocating work assignments and issuing deadlines, office and administrative support supervisors and managers oversee the work to ensure that it is proceeding on schedule and meeting established quality standards. This may involve reviewing each person's work on a computer—as in the case of accounting clerks—or listening to how a worker deals with customers—as in the case of customer services representatives. When supervising long-term projects, the supervisor may meet regularly with staff members to discuss their progress.

Office and administrative support supervisors and managers also evaluate each worker's performance. If a worker has done a good job, the supervisor indicates that in the employee's personnel file and may recommend a promotion or other award. Alternatively, if a worker is performing inadequately, the supervisor discusses the problem with the employee to determine the cause and helps the worker to improve his or her performance. This might require sending the employee to a training course or arranging personal counselling. If the situation does not improve, the supervisor may recommend a transfer, demotion, or dismissal.

Office and administrative support supervisors and managers usually interview and evaluate prospective employees. When new workers arrive on the job, supervisors greet them and provide orientation to acquaint them with their organization and its operating routines. Some supervisors may be actively involved in recruiting new workers—for example, by making presentations at high schools and business colleges. They also may serve as the primary liaisons between their offices and the general public through direct contact and by preparing promotional information.

Supervisors help train new employees in organization and office procedures. They may teach new employees how to use the telephone system and operate office equipment. Because most administrative support work is computerized, they also must teach new employees to use the organization's computer system. When new office equipment or updated computer software is introduced, supervisors train experienced employees to use it efficiently or, if this is not possible, arrange for their employees to receive special outside training.

Office and administrative support supervisors and managers often act as liaisons between the administrative support staff and the professional, technical and managerial staff. This may involve implementing new company policies or restructuring the workflow in their departments. They also must keep their superiors informed of their progress and any potential problems. Often, this communication takes the form of research projects and progress reports. Because supervisors and managers have access to information such as their department's performance records, they may compile and present these data for use in planning or designing new policies.

Office and administrative support supervisors and managers also may have to resolve interpersonal conflicts among the staff. In organizations covered by union contracts, supervisors must know the provisions of labour-management agreements and run their departments accordingly. They also may meet with union representatives to discuss work problems or grievances.

Working Conditions: Office and administrative support supervisors and managers are employed in a wide variety of work settings, but most work in clean and well-lit offices that usually are comfortable.

Most office and administrative support supervisors and managers work a standard 40-hour week. However, because some organizations operate around the clock, supervisors may have to work nights, weekends and holidays. Sometimes, supervisors rotate among the three 8-hour shifts in a workday; in other cases, shifts are assigned on the basis of seniority.

Training, Other Qualifications and Advancement: Most firms fill office and administrative support supervisory and managerial positions by promoting office or administrative support workers from within their organizations. To become eligible for promotion to a supervisory position, administrative support workers must prove they are capable of handling additional responsibilities. When evaluating candidates, supervisors look for strong teamwork, problem-solving, leadership and communication skills, as well as determination, loyalty, poise and confidence. They also look for more specific supervisory attributes, such as the ability to organize and coordinate work efficiently, to set priorities and to motivate others. Increasingly, supervisors need a broad base of office skills coupled with personal flexibility to adapt to changes in organizational structure and move among departments when necessary.

In addition, supervisors must pay close attention to detail to identify and correct errors made by the staff they oversee. Good working knowledge of the organization's computer system also is an advantage. Many employers require post-secondary training—in some cases, an associate or even a bachelor's degree.

Administrative support workers with potential supervisory abilities may be given occasional supervisory assignments. To prepare for full-time supervisory duties, workers may attend in-house training or take courses in time management, project management, or interpersonal relations. Some office and administrative support supervisor positions are filled with people from outside the organization. These positions may serve as entry-level training for potential higher level managers. New college graduates may rotate through departments of an organization at this level to learn the work of the organization.

Employment: Office and administrative support supervisors and managers held 1.5 million jobs in 2004. Although jobs for office and administrative support supervisors and managers are found in practically every industry, the largest number are found in organizations with a large administrative support workforce, such as banks, wholesalers, government agencies, retail establishments, business service firms, health care facilities, schools and insurance companies. Because of most organizations' need for continuity of supervision, few office and administrative support supervisors and managers work on a temporary or part-time basis.

Job Outlook: Like those seeking other supervisory and managerial occupations, applicants for jobs as office and administrative support worker supervisors and managers are likely to encounter keen competition because the number of applicants should greatly exceed the number of job openings. Employment is expected to grow more slowly than average for all occupations through 2014. Besides the job openings arising from growth, a large number of openings will stem from the need to replace workers who transfer to other occupations or leave this large occupation for other reasons.

Employment of office and administrative support supervisors and managers is determined largely by the demand for administrative support workers. New technology should increase office and administrative support workers' productivity and allow a wider variety of tasks to be performed by people in professional positions. These trends will cause employment in some administrative support occupations to grow slowly or even decline. As a result, supervisors will direct smaller permanent staffs—supplemented by increased use of temporary administrative support staff—and perform more professional tasks. Office and administrative support managers will coordinate the increasing amount of administrative work and make sure that the technology is applied and running properly. However, organizational restructuring should continue to reduce employment in some managerial positions, distributing more responsibility to office and administrative support supervisors.

Earnings: Median annual earnings of office and administrative support supervisors and managers were $41,030 in May 2004; the middle 50 percent earned between $31,860 and $53,110. The lowest paid 10 percent earned less than $25,190, while the highest paid 10 percent earned more than $67,800. In May 2004, median annual earnings in the industries employing the largest numbers of office and administrative support supervisors and managers were:

Insurance carriers	$49,610
Local government	42,100
State government	40,930
Offices of physicians	39,690
Depository credit intermediation	36,980

In addition to typical benefits, some office and administrative support supervisors and managers, particularly in the private sector, may receive additional compensation in the form of bonuses and stock options.

Librarianship

Libraries are repositories of knowledge, information and entertainment. The basic aim of library is to disseminate knowledge. With the upsurge in the number of institutes in the field of learning and the intensification of research activities, the importance of libraries is also growing. This has made the librarianship attain the status of a separate discipline in the universe of knowledge. Librarianship is the profession which concerns with organising, maintenance and storage of books in a library. Librarians are the custodians of library. Librarians assist people in finding information and using it effectively in their personal and professional lives. (They help people to navigate the increasingly far-flung and voluminous world of data.)

Libraries contain books, periodicals, micro-films, videos, cassettes and slides - for education, research, reference and pleasure. Those who systematically catalogue, store and display these items are librarians. The traditional concept of a library is being redefined, from a place to access paper records or books, to one which also houses the most advanced media, including CD-ROM, the Internet, virtual libraries and remote access to a wide range of resources. There are different kinds of libraries depending upon the individuals to which it is catering. Various kinds of libraries are public, reference, children's libraries and those attached to offices and institutions of both private and public. These could include a mobile lending library. There are also specialist libraries attached to the research and academic institutions that cater to specific readers in specific subjects such as medicine, engineering, art, music, or types of books such as Braille or collections for children.

Eligibility & Course Areas

Educational: Minimum qualification required to take up a course in Library Science is graduation. One with graduation can go for Bachelors degree in library science. Duration of this bachelors course is one year. Those with Bachelor degree in library science can go for Masters degree in library science which is of one year duration. One can also go for M.Phil and Ph.D in this field. There are also diploma and certificate courses.

Various universities, colleges, polytechnics, as well as distance learning institutions around the country offer courses in Library Science. In most of the institutes selection is through an entrance test. Course areas include library and information systems management, classification/cataloguing systems, bibliography, documentation, preservation and conservation of manuscript, library management, research methodology, computer applications, information processing, archives management, indexing, library planning etc.

Personal Attributes: One can become a librarian if he/she has a basic interest in books as well as a variety of topics, good communication skills, customer service attitude, methodical approach, organising ability, ability to anticipate user's needs, a wide general knowledge and ability to cope with frequent interruptions when doing jobs requiring concentration.

They must have knowledge of a wide variety of scholarly and public information sources and follow trends related to publishing, computers and the media to effectively oversee the selection and organization of library materials.

Job Prospects & Career Options

Job Prospects: Trained personnel in this field can find employment opportunities in areas like:

- Public/Government libraries
- Universities and other academic institutions
- News agencies and organisations
- Private organisations and special libraries
- Foreign embassies
- Photo/film libraries
- Information centres/documentation centres
- Companies and organisations with large information handling requirements

- Museums and galleries, which have reading rooms and research facilities

Some library technicians are self-employed as researchers, consultants, cataloguers etc. on short term contracts.

Career Options: Librarians are information managers. Librarians assist people in finding information and using it effectively. A librarian's work would involve acquiring, organising and dissemination of information. Besides these, the planning and coordination of the library's financial operations are also important and essential tasks to be performed. Specific duties depends on the type of library and position held.

Acquisition of knowledge/information involves selection, ordering and purchasing materials within the budget limits. For this one must have to take into consideration users interest and latest developments in various subjects to be able to maintain a balanced collection. Organising information involves classification, cataloguing, storage, record keeping, shelving and maintenance of books and materials in a manner so as to make it easily accessible to readers and users.

Dissemination of information is the most important work of the librarian, one that is very much directly related to users. A librarian thus disseminates information by answering queries, issuing and receiving books as well as planning and organising activities to encourage use of the library, like sending out a newsletter informing readers of the latest acquisitions, or inviting a children's author to read his/her book or sign autographs.

The career for a librarian may begin at the level of library attendant and though the promotions may differ from organization to organization, in general the levels followed thereafter are of library assistant, junior librarian, assistant librarian, deputy librarian and librarian. One may reach up to the level of Director and head an information centre.

Library Attendant: Takes care of inter-library loans shelving books, processing bills, subscription renewals and new memberships.

Library Assistant: Main duties involve accession, shelf arrangements, levying of fines, maintenance and binding of books and other materials, location of missing books and related technical work.

Junior Librarian/Semi-Professional Assistant: Works at the counter to receive and issue books, sends out reminders on overdue loans, looks after accessioning.

Junior Librarian/Professional Assistant: Is responsible for accessioning, classification, cataloguing, ordering books, as well as handling computer data.

Junior Librarian/Assistant Librarian: Selects and acquires books and material, takes care of reference services and computer programming, as well as supervision of semi-professional assistants.

Deputy Librarian: Oversees administration, supervision and computer programming.

Librarian: Is overall in charge of technical, administrative and financial matters. Responsibilities include delegation of duties, library supervision and management, personnel administration, budgeting, classification and cataloguing and recommendation of new acquisitions.

Director/Head of Information Centre: Works at the policy and planning level and is responsible for the center's organization, coordination, control, leadership, external relations, supervision and administration.

In information services, designations could be:

Senior Information Analyst: Activities include processing of information, indexing, documentation etc.

Junior Information Analyst: Assists senior analyst in all aspects of work.

Information Assistant: Information transfers, processing, storage and dissemination of information under supervision of senior staff are the main tasks in this position.

Remuneration: Salaries of librarians vary according to the individual's qualifications, experience, type, size and the nature of the hiring institutions. Librarians with primarily administrative duties often have greater earnings. Government of India scales are higher than those of the University Grants Commission. In terms of grades- Assistant Librarians are of equal position to lecturers; Deputy Librarians to Readers; and the Librarian's position is equivalent to that of a Professor's. Average annual earnings of librarians is around Rs 100000 - 150000.

Library or Information Science: Today, information resources go far beyond the traditional printed word. Electronic databases, the Internet and CD-ROMs join published material and audiovisual resources in an increasingly crowded information environment. It is the library and its staff which form the vital link between the vast body of information and the people who need it. Library staff are knowledge managers in a knowledge hungry universe.

Libraries aren't the only places you'll find information experts these days. People skilled in information delivery work in all kinds of settings. Their skills in management, communication, organization, systems design and information classification are in demand in fields such as archives, records management and systems analysis. Many graduates adapt their training to successful careers as webmasters, consultants, sales and marketing coordinators or entrepreneurs.

Educational programmes in library and information sciences produce graduates with varying levels of expertise. The following descriptions outline the positions normally encountered in the library field. Librarians hold a minimum of two post-secondary degrees: an undergraduate degree with a subject specialty and a postgraduate degree in library or information science, or information studies. As information specialists, they understand and are skilled in:

- defining information needs;
- methods of information seeking and communication;
- assessing the relevance of information;
- managing information services in any context;
- assisting patrons to use the most common information tools in the most appropriate fashion;

- archiving;
- records management;
- readers advisory services

They plan, develop and coordinate all aspects of library and information services. Librarians have the expertise to select, acquire and catalogue a wide range of library materials, including books, journals, government information, audio and video materials as well as electronic information resources. Graduates of library and information studies programmes are often at the forefront of developments in information technology.

At the management level, they set goals, establish policies, prepare budgets and organize staff to meet the information needs of their organizations. Library Technicians are graduates of a library diploma programme offered by a community college or technical institute. Their training prepares them to perform the specialized functions unique to the library or information environment, preparing them to support and assist librarians, coordinate the work of the clerical staff or, under the direction of a librarian, be responsible for a section or department in a larger library. Duties may vary with the type and size of the library but can include: acquiring print and nonprint material, cataloguing and classifying of the materials, producing graphic and display materials and circulation procedures. In a small library, where the foundations of organization and operation are already established, the library technician may serve as the library manager.

Library Assistants often hold one or more university degrees with subject specialization outside of the library field. Their role is to assist the professional librarian or information specialist, in tasks such as selection and organization of materials in their subject specialty, as well as assisting library customers with research. Their education gives them subject expertise, familiarity with research techniques and a broad base of knowledge. They build on this academic foundation as they gain library experience. They may also participate in acquisitions and technical services in ordering, processing and cataloguing materials or work in the area of public services to patrons, charging out or receiving materials.

Library Clerks perform routine tasks such as shelving books and periodicals, signing out material or maintaining books and equipment. Many clerks use their typing and computer skills to process materials orders and to update library catalogues. They work under the direction of staff trained in the library and information profession. High school graduation is generally required and standard secretarial and computer skills are highly desirable.

Teacher Librarians are fully qualified teachers, who typically undertake postgraduate education in library studies. They work in partnership with classroom teachers to provide a wide range of learning resources to students in the elementary and secondary school environments; to plan, teach and evaluate instructional programmes; to promote literacy among students; develop library collections; and supervise support staff.

Traditional or Non-Traditional Library Careers Working in a public, academic, school or government library would be considered a traditional library career.

Increasingly, however, graduates from library and information science programmes are choosing non-traditional paths. This new breed can be found working in publishing or for companies that supply goods and services to libraries. Some become web masters, independent information consultants or start their own information-related business. They may hold management positions in associations or corporate positions like electronic image manager or risk management researcher. The possibilities grow yearly, as emerging information technologies create a need for more information specialists.

Salaries: Information about library salaries can be found in the CASLIS (Canadian Association of Special Libraries and Information Services) Salary Survey, 1998. ISBN 0-88802- 290-5. $52.00. To order the Salary Survey, contact CLA .

Library Education in America

This directory provides information about library and information studies programmes that are accredited by the American Library Association (ALA). The ALA Office for Accreditation publishes the directory annually and provides the opportunity for programmes to update their entries online when information changes.

Each entry includes contact information, the name of the accredited programme, date through which it is accredited and distance education opportunities. If you have any questions about a programme, please contact the programme directly. ALA accredits master's programmes in the U.S., Canada and Puerto Rico only. Programmes are listed alphabetically by the state or province in which the primary campus is located. There is an index by institution at the end of the directory.

Some entries have a notation of (Conditional) next to them. This indicates conditional accreditation-a status assigned to a programme that must make changes to comply with the 1992 Standards for Accreditation of Master's Programmes in Library and Information Studies to enable accreditation beyond the date specified by the Committee on Accreditation (COA). Please note that these programmes are fully accredited under the Standards.

The directory includes LIS distance education offerings available at each programme. Programmes may offer distance education through traditional extension programmes with faculty on-site or through interactive video, the Internet, or other technologies. Prospective students should verify with the programme the extent to which a full master's programme can be completed off-site. Distance education offerings change frequently, so prospective students should inquire with the programme for the most current information.

"Guidelines for Choosing a Master's Programme in Library and Information Studies" is designed to help prospective students select a programme. For more detailed information, prospective students should visit the website and request catalogues and applications from programmes in which they are interested.

Library and Information Studies

Prospective students should consider several factors when choosing a graduate programme for a master's degree in library and information studies. These include both personal and professional considerations such as career plans, interest in various specializations, geographic mobility, distance learning opportunities and financial resources. These guidelines suggest some information gathering techniques to assist prospective students in choosing a programme.

The master's degree in library and information studies is frequently referred to as the MLS; however, ALA-accredited programmes offer degrees with names such as Master of Arts, Master of Librarianship, Master of Library and Information Studies, or Master of Science. The ALA Office for Human Resource Development and Recruitment offers information on careers in library and information studies and on selecting an ALA-accredited programme.

Accreditation: Graduating from an ALA-accredited programme enhances your career mobility and provides greater flexibility in the types of libraries, information centres and jobs for which you can apply. The majority of employers require an ALA-accredited master's for professional positions. Some states require an ALA-accredited degree to work as a professional librarian in public or school libraries.

ALA accredits master's programmes in library and information studies in the United States, Canada and Puerto Rico. ALA policy recognizes the ALA-accredited master's degree as the appropriate professional degree for librarians and information professionals. For school library media specialists, a master's degree with a specialty in school library media from an educational unit accredited by the National Council for the Accreditation of Teacher Education (NCATE) is also appropriate. ALA's policy states that "The master's degree in librarianship from a programme accredited by the American Library Association or a master's degree with a specialty in school library media from an educational unit accredited by the National Council for the Accreditation of Teacher Education is the appropriate first professional degree." (ALA Policy 54.2.2)

ALA accreditation indicates that the programme has undergone a self-evaluation process, been reviewed by peers and meets the Standards for Accreditation of Master's Programmes in Library and Information Studies that were established by the Committee on Accreditation and adopted by the ALA Council in 1992. The Committee on Accreditation evaluates each programme for conformity to the Standards, which address mission, goals and objectives, curriculum, faculty, students, administration and financial support and physical resources and facilities.

Gathering Basic Information: Although all programmes accredited by ALA's COA meet the Standards, there is a considerable diversity among programmes. We encourage prospective students to contact programmes directly for specific information. To help in your decision we suggest that you review the programme's web site; talk to the faculty, students and alumni; and ask librarians in your area to answer questions about your specific interests and concerns.

To get the latest information about the programmes in which you are interested, visit the programme's web site or request a print catalogue. These resources provide information on the programme's mission, goals and objectives, curriculum, current and future course schedules, application deadlines and admission requirements and procedures.

Visiting the schools you are considering can help you select the programme that best meets your goals. While you are on-site, investigate university facilities such as computer and library resources. The general campus environment, availability of affordable on-campus housing or housing near the university, child care facilities and extra-curricular activities may be important to some prospective students. If you notify a programme of your intention to visit, meetings can be arranged with administrators, faculty members and/or students.

The ALA's Office for Human Resource Development and Recruitment web site also provides links to many resources to help you obtain information when selecting a programme. At this site you will find information on scholarships, placement, salaries and general career information.

Admission Requirements: Individual institutions and programmes establish their own admission requirements, which vary from programme to programme. Generally, programmes require a bachelor's degree from a regionally accredited institution and a minimum grade point average of 3.0 on a 4.0 scale (or equivalent, *e.g.*, B average). Many programmes require Graduate Record Examination (GRE) scores; a few accept the Miller Analogies Test or have no test requirements. Students from outside the United States may be required to take The Test of English as a Foreign Language (TOEFL). Most programmes request that students provide several letters of recommendation and a statement of educational and professional objectives. Some programmes may also require a personal interview. Entering students may be required to demonstrate computer skills or successful completion of remedial computer courses early in the programme.

Curriculum: Considerable variation exists in curricula offered by the programmes, such as the number and types of required courses. The number of academic credit hours required for a master's degree also varies from 36 semester hours to 72 quarter hours. Some programmes emphasize full-time studies, while others have a larger percentage of part-time students; however, most have a time limit for completing a degree.

Many programmes can be completed in one calendar year with full-time attendance; some require two academic years to complete the programme. Programmes requiring a thesis or practicum may require more time to complete.

Choosing a Specialization: Some students enter a master's programme knowing what they want to do when they graduate, some have not made a decision and some see their interests shift once they are exposed to the wide variety of types and settings in which librarians and information professionals work. Plan a programme of study based on an assessment of your past experiences, education, personal strengths and interests, geographic mobility, intended career path and future plans. Although you should be aware of job market opportunities, you should not necessarily let them dictate your choice to specialize. Faculty advisors can help in the process of developing a programme of study that fits your needs.

All ALA-accredited programmes have required courses to provide general preparation to practice in the profession. Some programmes also offer specialized tracks or courses that permit or encourage concentration in a specific area of library and information studies (for example, school librarianship, art librarianship, health science librarianship, database design, or archives). The opportunity to specialize depends on the availability of relevant courses, on focused class project/paper opportunities and the availability of practica or student employment options.

Flexibility and Distance Learning: Flexibility in fulfilling course requirements may be important to students who work or live away from a campus or in an area that does not have an ALA-accredited programme. Most programmes allow students to take independent studies, courses in other schools, graduate departments, or universities and apply the credits towards the master's in library and information studies.

Many ALA-accredited programmes provide distance-learning opportunities for students through a variety of delivery methods. In some cases students can complete the entire programme can be at a distance; in other cases some on-campus courses or regional residency may be required. Because these offerings change very frequently, prospective students should contact the programme directly for the latest information on distance learning options.

Financial Aid: Financial aid can consist of scholarships, teaching and research assistantships, grants, work-study programmes, loans and tuition assistance. The programme administers some financial aid opportunities while others are administered through the general university financial aid office. There may be reciprocal tuition agreements between states that can reduce tuition or provide tuition waivers. In addition, some employers provide tuition assistance as a fringe benefit to employees.

Prospective students should contact the institution and programme to obtain information on financial aid and scholarships. In addition to work-study, other part-time positions may be available at local area libraries or information settings. Work in an information setting not only helps finance your education-it also provides valuable experience.

Financial Assistance for Library and Information Studies, an annual compilation available from the ALA Committee on Education, provides listings of financial aid from a variety of sources. In Canada, prospective students should also contact the Canadian Library Association.

Scholarship application deadlines vary and may be as early as a year in advance of the term of enrollment.

Placement Services

Most programmes offer some type of job placement service for both current students and alumni. Some have a designated placement officer, while others use faculty for job search advising. Most programmes receive job listings from around the country, although some programmes may be better able to help graduates find jobs in the local area. You may wish to inquire to the programme about placement statistics to learn about the types of jobs obtained by recent graduates. The ALA Office for Human Resource Development and Recruitment web site also provides information on placement, salaries and general career information.

The job market for library and information professionals is cyclical and varies by type of institution, job function and geographical area. The availability of positions may be dependent on available funding resources and replacement needs. Many graduates also find positions in settings other than traditional libraries; these may include special libraries, software or hardware development companies, information management firms, indexing and abstracting agencies and information technology firms.

How Can I Learn about Law Librarianship as a Career?

What do law librarians do? Law librarians are professionally trained people who work in various legal settings, including law schools, private law firms and government libraries.

The American Association of Law Libraries (AALL) has published a booklet, entitled "Finding Your Way in the Information Age" that explains the many roles of law librarians as well as the kinds of skills needed to be successful in this profession. You can request a free copy from AALL.

If you are interested in learning about the profession, you should also look at the two major publications of the American Association of Law Libraries, AALL Spectrum and the Law Library Journal. AALL is a professional organization representing 5,000 law librarians. The association exists to promote and enhance the value of law libraries to the public, the legal community and the world; to foster the profession of law librarianship; and to provide leadership in the field of legal information. A review of AALLNET will help you understand this profession and the kinds of work we do.

We recommend that you talk to librarians in the field about the profession. Contact your local law school library, law firm, or local public law library. Most law librarians will be happy to talk to you about our profession and answer your questions. Many large cities and several regions of the country have local organizations of law librarians, called AALL chapters. Communicate with them to identify law librarians to talk with; attend their meetings; educate yourself!

What are the Academic Qualifications for a Law Librarian?

There are several different routes to take to obtain the education needed to work as a law librarian. 85% of those working as law librarians have a graduate degree in library science. Most jobs require a master's degree from an American Library Association (ALA) accredited institution. The names of the degrees vary MLS, MLIS, MSIS, ML, MA in LS but all reflect an appropriate entry level educational requirement for careers in the law librarianship profession.

Nearly 30% of all law librarians also have a JD or LLB degree. Most positions require that this degree be earned from a law school accredited by the American Bar Association (ABA).

Less than 20% of the law librarian jobs being filled require both degrees. (National searches are routinely conducted by academic law libraries so most academic jobs will be posted on the webpage. Conversely, the sectors where law degrees are rarely required most often do not search nationally, so most of those jobs are not advertised through the national sources like AALLNET.)

Some jobs will require the graduate degree in library science but state a preference for the law degree as well. Experience working in a law library is often as important as having a law degree.

Several schools offer a joint JD/MLS degree where a student can earn a law degree and a library degree simultaneously. Check with the individual school to understand the number of credit hours required. Most of these programmes will require at least 4 years of study.

In sum, to qualify for virtually any professional job in law libraries you must have a graduate degree in library science. You may want to consider also earning your law degree. Armed with JD and MLS degrees, you will be qualified for more positions in law librarianship.

Typically, directors of academic law libraries have faculty status so they must have a law degree. In addition, many (but not all) reference librarian positions in law schools require a law degree. Ordinarily, there is no law degree requirement for law librarian positions in law firms, corporations or public, county and government law libraries.

If you already have a law degree but no graduate library degree, should you invest in another 1-2 years of professional education? From the surveys done in the law librarianship profession and from close examination of the job postings for the last few years, a law degree alone would rarely qualify you for jobs in any kind of law library. There are some exceptions, especially if you are interested in eventually obtaining the library degree. The best advice is to encourage you to get the graduate library science degree. On its face you will be qualified for many more positions in law libraries. In addition, you will be much better prepared to assume the challenges and changes of librarianship in today and tomorrow's environment.

How do I Evaluate Library and Information Science Programmes for a Career in Law Librarianship?

You have many factors to consider when evaluating a graduate programme in library and information science, including the location of the school, tuition and cost of living and your ultimate career goals. There are many fine ALA approved institutions that offer a master's degree in library and information science (often designated as an MLS or MLIS). Today, there are fifty-one accredited programmes to choose from. You may also be interested in the top twenty library schools as ranked by US News.

However, in selecting the library science programme that you think will meet your needs for a career in law librarianship, you will also need some subject specialization in the law. The AALL Guidelines for Graduate Programmes suggest that you will need both general competencies and subject competencies.

General competencies include reference and research services, library management, collection management and organization and classification. These competencies can be obtained through any of the various library and information science schools.

Subject competencies include an understanding of the legal system; a knowledge of the legal profession and its terminology, including legal abbreviations and citation systems; a knowledge of the literature of the law, including the legal documents that are published and issued by the various branches of government; and an understanding of the legal requirements and ethical considerations of the legal profession and librarianship. You will find a list of thirty-one competencies for law librarian professionals titled "Credentialing Survey Confirms Law Librarian Competencies and Training Needs" in the April, 1998 issue of AALL Spectrum. These competencies were identified on the AALL Credentialing Survey and provide a solid core of what law librarians do.

These law-related subject competencies can be obtained in several ways. Locate a graduate programme in library science that offers courses in law librarianship. Some schools offer one course, others offer two courses and others offer more in-depth study by offering at least three courses. While a graduate programme that offers only one course in law librarianship does not give you an in depth exposure to law librarianship, you may be able to supplement the course with independent studies, internships for academic credit that give you experience working in a law library, or work in a law library while you are in school. Presently, some library schools do not offer any courses in law librarianship, however, this situation could change and you should check directly with the school.

The Special Libraries Association issued a Library and Information Studies Programmes Survey which compares the competencies developed for special librarians and the corresponding courses that are offered in graduate library programmes.

View a complete list of the graduate programmes in library and information science with some offering coursework in law librarianship. You may also be interested in the top twenty library schools as ranked by US News, which now also ranks programmes in law librarianship.

What are the Admission Requirements for Graduate Schools of Library and Information Science?

Admission requirements vary from school to school, but most schools generally require a bachelor's degree and a minimum grade point average (usually a B). Many programmes also require a minimum score on the Graduate Record Examination (GRE); some have no test requirements or will take test scores from alternative examinations, such as the Law School Admission Test (LSAT) or the Miller Analogies Test. Many schools require letters of recommendation and some hold personal interviews or request a statement of educational objectives from the applicant. Most schools also require a basic level of proficiency in the use of computers. Be sure to check the individual school's website for more specific information about admission requirements, especially application deadlines.

What Type of Curriculum Should I Expect?

Many masters programmes in Library and Information Science can be completed in one calendar year with full-time attendance, but the number of academic credit hours required for a master's degree varies from school to school. Some programmes can take as long as two years and may require a thesis and/or fieldwork. Most schools permit part-time attendance and many now have some distance education opportunities. According to the Association for Library and Information Science Education's Statistical Report for 1998, forty-two (75%) of the library schools offered one or more distance courses in 1996-97. No two library science distance education programmes are exactly alike, for they offer various methods of delivery: e-mail, satellite transmission, correspondence courses and the Internet.

Check the breadth and depth of their law librarianship course offerings. A group of law librarians known as the Conference of Law Library Educators teach courses in library schools. Syllabi for many courses offered in law librarianship can be found on their webpage.

Law librarians must have skills in legal research, legal bibliography, organization of legal materials, law library administration and knowledge of legal information systems. Most graduate programmes focus on technology's role in storing and accessing information, or offer coursework in understanding and utilizing the latest technology. A good foundation in technology is essential for law librarianship. Law librarians should be familiar with online databases, such as WESTLAW, LEXIS and Dialog. Law Librarians must be able to help patrons obtain desired information and facilitate access to library material through cataloging and classification.

You may want to look at the course offerings in other academic departments of the University you are considering. Internship and fieldwork opportunities are also an important consideration. You may also want to look at the school's computer and technical resources, such as the size and hours of the computer lab and the number and types of courses offered in online technology and information system management. Check out the school's placement or career services department? How will they help you get a job after you earn your degree?

As with any other profession, competition is fierce for well-paying jobs and you should acquire as many marketable skills as possible.

How Can I Finance a Degree in Library and Information Science?

The American Association of Law Libraries is committed to providing opportunities for professional growth. Each year, the Association awards scholarships in significant amounts to students seeking formal education in law or librarianship and who can demonstrate financial need. The Special Libraries Association (SLA) and ALA also award many scholarships each year. In addition, the newly created Gates Millennium Scholarship Programme targets the field of library science among other fields.

List of Library and Information Science Programmes

Africa:

- University of Natal
- University of South Africa

Asia:

- University Teknologi Mara Faculty of Information Management
- University of Hong Kong, Master of Science in Library and Information Management (MSc.[LIM])
- Chiang Mai University
- Chonnam National University
- Chulalongkorn University
- Jilin University
- Nanjing University
- Nankai University
- North Sumatra University, Medan, Indonesia
- Padjadjaran University, Bandung, Indonesia
- Peking University
- Sichuan University
- Sun Yat-sen University
- Wuhan University
- Xiangtan University
- Yonsei University
- University of Indonesia, Jakarta, Indonesia
- University of the Philippines, Diliman
  - o Institute of Library and Information Science

Australia:

- Charles Sturt University, School of Information Studies
- Curtin University, School of Computer and Information Science
- Edith Cowan University, School of Computer and Information Science
- Monash University, School of Information Management and Systems
- RMIT University, School of Business Information Technology
- Queensland University of Technology, School of Information Systems
- University of South Australia, School of Communication, Information and New Media
- University of Technology Sydney, Faculty of Humanities and Social Sciences

India:

- Department of Library and Information Science, Madurai Kamaraj University, Madurai, Tamil Nadu
- Department of Library and Information Science, University of Kerala
- Indian Statistical Institute, Documentation Research and Training Centre
- University of Mumbai, Department of Library and Information Science
- Bhavnagar University

Canada:

- University of Alberta School of Library and Information Studies
- McGill University Graduate School of Library and Information Studies
- University of Western Ontario, Faculty of Information & Media Studies
- University of Toronto, Faculty of Information Studies (Toronto)

- Dalhousie University, School of Information Management
- University of British Columbia, School of Library, Archival and Information Studies
- University de Montreal, Ecole de bibliotheconomie et des sciences de linformation (EBSI)

Europe:

- Abo Akademi University, Department of Information Studies
- University College, London, School of Library, Archive and Information Studies
- University of Oulu, Department of Finnish, Information Studies and Logopedics
- University of Tampere, Department of Information Studies
- University of Amsterdam, Department of Information Science
- Danmarks Bibliothesskole / Royal School of Library and Information Science
- University of Antwerp, Department of Library and Information Science
- Université Libre de Bruxelles, Master en Sciences et technologies de Iinformation et de la communication
- City University, London, Department of Information Science
- University of Sheffield, Department of Information Studies
- University of Strathclyde, Glasgow, Department of Computer and Information Sciences, Graduate School of Informatics
- Robert Gordon University, Aberdeen, Department of Information Management
- University of Wales, Aberystwyth, Department of Information Studies

Middle East

Iran:

- University of Tehran, Department of Library & Information Science

- Ferdowsi University of Mashhad, Department of Library and Information Studies
- Shahid Chamran University, Department of Library & Information Science
- Shiraz University, Department of Library & Information Science
- Tarbiat Modaress University, Department of Library & Information Science

Pakistan:

- University of the Punjab
- University of Karachi
- Islamia University
- Bahauddin Zakariya University
- Allama Iqbal Open University
- Peshawar University.

United States:

- The Catholic University of America, School of Library and Information Science
- Clarion University of Pennsylvania, Clarion, Pennsylvania, Department of Library Science
- Dominican University, River Forest, Illinois, Graduate School of Library and Information Science
- Emporia State University, Emporia, Kansas, School of Library and Information Management
- Florida State University, Tallahassee, Florida, College of Information
- Indiana University, School of Library and Information Science
- Kent State University, School of Library and Information Science
- Long Island University Palmer School of Library and Information Science
- Louisiana State University School of Library and Information Science
- North Carolina Central University, School of Library and Information Science

- Pratt Institute, Manhattan campus, School of Information and Library Science
- Queens College, City University of New York
- Rutgers The State University, New Brunswick, New Jersey, School of Communication, Information and Library Studies
- San Jose State University, San Jose, California, School of Library and Information Science.
- Simmons College, Boston, Massachusetts, Graduate School of Library & Information Science
- Southern Connecticut State University, Information and Library Science Programme
- Syracuse University, School of Information Studies
- Texas Woman's University, Denton, Texas, School of Library and Information Studies
- University of Alabama, Tuscaloosa, Alabama Alabama School of Library and Information Studies
- University at Albany, State University of New York School of Information Science & Policy
- University at Buffalo, State University of New York
- University of Arizona, School of Information Resources and Library Science
    - Digital Library of Information Science and Technology
- University of California, Los Angeles UCLA Graduate School of Education and Information Studies
- University of Hawaii at Manoa Library and Information Science Programme
- University of Illinois Graduate School of Library and Information Science
- University of Maryland, College Park, College of Information Studies
- University of Michigan, Ann Arbor, Michigan, School of Information
- University of North Carolina at Chapel Hill School of Information and Library Science

- University of North Carolina at Greensboro School of Library and Information Studies
- University of North Texas, Denton, Texas, School of Library and Information Sciences
- University of Pittsburgh School of Information Sciences
- University of South Florida School of Library and Information Science
- University of Tennessee at Knoxville School of Information Sciences
- University of Texas at Austin School of Information Sciences
- University of Washington Information School
- University of Rhode Island Graduate School of Library and Information Studies
- University of Wisconsin-Madison, School of Library and Information Sciences
- University of Wisconsin-Milwaukee, School of Information Studies
- Wayne State University, Detroit, Michigan, Library and Information Science Programme

Education Schools and Library Schools

The library profession has long been concerned by the lack of esteem that higher education has regarded library education. The closing of more than a dozen graduate programmes in library science from the late 70s to the early 90s raised this concern to an even higher level. Many librarians assumed that higher education as a whole had no respect for librarianship when the most prestigious and well-regarded library schools at Columbia and Chicago were closed. Librarians are not alone in being taken lightly by the academy.

Teacher educators also have had to struggle with the low opinions of their fellow faculty on campus. Examining education schools and library schools reveals many similarities between them in regards to status in higher education and may shed new light on the issue for interested members of each profession.

The issues involved in low status on campus for education and library schools are many and varied. No paper can hope to embrace the full scale of this problem. The issues include such matters as gender and class bias, low pay, the nature of the knowledge studied and factors inherent to schools and libraries such as their public nature and the easy look of the professions. This paper is not an attempt to thoroughly examine all angles and suggest solutions. This paper is an attempt to compare the similarities of education and library schools in regards to status. To the knowledge of this author, this has not been attempted before.

The Image Problem of Education and Library Schools: The bulk of this article will deal with exploring why education and library schools are so poorly received on campus and what has been written in response to this problem. However, a brief review of the problem is in order before starting on the whys. Both education and library educators are viewed poorly on most higher education campuses. This has led to faculty in these schools being looked down on by other faculty on campus, being paid far less than comparable faculty in other fields and it has led to in the case of library schools closings.

It is easiest to discuss the low esteem is in the case of library schools. Universities are making a real effort to eliminate library schools. If universities valued library schools, they would not close them. Wrote White, "A serious threat to library education comes from our academic colleagues, who do not know us, do not appreciate us and do not understand us." This statement seems hard to dispute as library schools continue to close.

The lack of academic prestige has hurt library schools in a major way. There have never been an abundance of library schools in the United States. Now there are less than sixty. Library schools have closed at Alabama A&M, Ball State, California State at Fullerton, Case Western Reserve, Columbia, Chicago, the University of Denver, Emory University, the University of Minnesota, the University of Mississippi, the State University of New York at Geneseo, Oregon, Southern California, Vanderbilt and Western Michigan in the last twenty years. The programmes at Chicago and Columbia were considered the best in the field. Their closure meant that the quality of the programmes was not the problem. The problem was that they were library schools and the university did not want them.

Many library writers believe that library schools have been closed because administrators needed to show that they were financially responsible to trustees and state legislators. White and Paris both take this view. Library schools were small, lacked prestige and had few allies in the state legislature to defend them. Closing the schools saved little money. Yet, it allowed the administration to show that they were belt tightening. The administrators could not close other programmes that perhaps could have saved money. These programmes were too prestigious and too powerful. The library school thus became the sacrificial victim. The fact that this has happened repeatedly across higher education is a pretty clear indication that library schools (and by extension librarians) are not valued highly by the academy.

The case for the low status of education schools is harder to make. Few education schools have been closed. It is unlikely that many education schools will be closed in the future. Yet, education school faculties are constantly under attack not only on campus but also by society as a whole. No other discipline on campus draws the criticism that education schools do. Something (or multiple something's as the bulk of this paper will cover) makes society and academia dislike education schools.

The Gourman Report on Graduate Programmes (1996) is a book that evaluates and ranks programmes in every academic discipline. The report has been criticized heavily by librarians because it refuses to reveal how it evaluates programmes. Of interest is that education is one of only two fields (the other is criminal justice) that the report writes is worthless. The book goes on in great detail to describe all programmes of education as being without any redeeming academic value. It concludes that all education programmes at all institutions of higher education should be abolished. It then lists every programme of education in the United States and page by page gives each one a 0 evaluation. (It is interesting to note that library science is considered "Real" by Mr. Gourman. However, his book lists the Columbia University programme as being number 1 in the United States even though the programme closed several years before the latest edition of his book was published.) This book is popular and used by many in higher education to compare programmes. It is particularly popular with students. Yet, every edition of the book completely trashes all education schools. It is hard to imagine medicine, philosophy, law, biology, or most other fields getting this kind of treatment from a well-known reference book. There is something different about the general view of education schools that is being reflected here.

On campus, even associating with education schools can get a faculty member in trouble. Wrote Lanier and Little, "It is common knowledge that professors in the arts and sciences risk a loss of academic respect, including promotion and tenure, if they assume clear interest in or responsibility for teacher education." It is hard to imagine faculty getting in serious trouble for associating with other fields. Cross-disciplinary collaborations are usually welcome on most campuses. Again, the question arises, why is education getting such different treatment?

Perhaps the best way that education schools are viewed on campus is summed up by David Labaree. He wrote, "The university views colleges of education as nothing but trade schools, which provides vocational training but no academic curriculum." The university wants the money that the education school brings in. Yet, it does not respect the expertise that the education school has. It is tolerated because it is necessary but few respect it. And, like library schools, they are constantly under attack. Why does the academy have such low esteem for education and library schools?

Reasons for Low Esteem in Higher Education: It is difficult if not impossible to give a single reason as to why faculty in education and library schools are not viewed as the equals of other faculty on campus. This is due to the fact that many different factors are influencing this belief. No one may consciously recognize any of the factors when considering education and library faculty but these factors have almost certainly shaped the beliefs and views of those in higher education. Gender bias towards women appears to be a factor as both education and library science are fields dominated by women. The low to moderate pay that most teachers and librarians receive is also a factor as education and library school alumni have less incomes to donate to the higher education institutions that they graduated from. Social bias may play a part as many teacher and library educators come from working class backgrounds in contrast to more privileged backgrounds for many other faculty. The tendency for education and librarianship to focus on practical rather than theoretical matters also does not sit well with faculty in more theoretical disciplines. Finally, the public nature of schools and libraries leads many to believe that education and library faculties have no special knowledge that any one could not learn independently.

Unfortunately, society does not regard work done by women as important as work done by men. This gender bias has lead to wage gap between men and women that has women making considerably less than men in the United States. Those professional fields dominated by women (librarianship, teaching and nursing for example) make less money than those professional fields dominated by men. Because education and library school faculties teach primarily women, they are subject to this bias. Perhaps unwittingly, other faculty do not value those who labour to teach women about subject matter which is seen as feminine. Attacks on teacher education and the closings of library schools could well be manifestations of continued gender bias in higher education.

Related to gender bias, the low pay of teachers and librarians hurts education and library schools. Most beginning teachers and librarians make less than thirty thousand dollars a year. Few librarians or teachers ever make more than fifty thousand dollars a year unless they move into administration. Even teacher and librarian administrators make less than administrators do in other fields. This has a very real effect on education and library schools. Alumni of these programmes have less income that they can devote to donating to their alma mater. This then gives education and library schools less political power on campus in relation to other academic departments who have graduates making more money and donating more of it to the higher education institution. Of course, teachers and librarians make less because each is a field dominated by women, so this skewing of academic power in favour of departments with higher income graduates is yet another manifestation of gender bias in higher education.

The role of social bias can not be overlooked either. Wrote Prichard et al, "A much larger number of incumbents enter the field of college teaching of education from homes of skilled and unskilled labourers than have been found for incumbents in other areas of academic work." While this study is over 25 years old, the conclusions still are true today. Teaching and librarianship are much easier for the children of the working class to break into than most other professional fields. Becoming a teacher or librarians takes less time and costs less than becoming a doctor or lawyer for example. Most education and library school faculty started as teachers and librarians before moving into higher education faculty roles. They share this blue-collar background in most cases. Faculty in other fields tend to come from more privileged backgrounds. This sets faculty in education and librarianship apart from their peers.

Education schools and library schools are also scorned by other higher education faculty for their focus on practical rather than theoretical knowledge. Education and library literature are full of examples of "how I teach good" and "how I run my library good" articles. Even more research-oriented articles tend to have a practical component to them as well they should. Yet, these types of articles do not garner respect from the vast majority of faculty who focus on theoretical knowledge and let others draw the practicality from this knowledge. Wrote Labaree, "In the commodified setting of US education, usable knowledge is low-status knowledge. The more knowledge is removed from ordinary concerns and the more closely associated it is with high culture, the more prestige it carries." Yet, education and library knowledge needs to be usable. No one wants teachers and librarians who are unprepared to do their jobs. This has not helped the image of education and library school faculty despite this need.

There is also some resistance to doing research in education school faculty and it is probably safe to write in library school faculty as well. Ducharme and Agne wrote that education faculty "have difficulty in adjusting to and accepting the norms and expectations of academe." This usually takes the form of resistance to doing research and publishing in peer-reviewed journals. The two researchers traced this back to the working class origin of education school faculty. Failing to emulate the academic lifestyle properly is a hindrance to education and library school faculty. Of course, it begs the larger question of how much these faculty should emulate the academic model.

All of the previous reasons are part of why librarianship and education have image problems in higher education. However, the root of the problem may come down to two reasons. The public ultimately controls both schools and libraries and most everyone feels entitled to venture their opinion on how to run them. Faculty in the majority of other disciplines are considered the authorities in their fields and the public does not expect to question them. In addition, most faculty in higher education learned to teach by teaching. They never went through a formal education on how to teach. These faculty can then imagine that education is a simple field if they could master it without having attended an education school. Although the average faculty member does not acquire considerable library experience, it is easy to imagine that most higher education faculty believe they are qualified to run a library.

The accessibility and public ownership of education is one of its biggest assets and perhaps largest liability in higher education. Wrote Cusick, "Individual freedom runs all the way through the system. Parents may or may not support the school board; superintendents may support or oppose the state department, state department staff may alter the intent of federal policy makers. People make and exercise personal decisions, enter and take part on their own terms and regards those as their rights. Students mix their classes, cultures and friendships with school requirements; teachers adjust their curriculums to their predilections, create their student relations and support or oppose principals as they choose. Reformers decide schools need accountability, or principals decide their teachers have too much or too little power. Teachers decide students need more freedom. Each member of the system is free to make his or her own decision and set a course of action."

It is precisely for this reason that education schools and library schools are not considered intellectually rigorous. Everyone in society including the student, the politician and the local businessman are allowed to have opinions on how schools and libraries ought to be ran and expect to voice these opinions whenever they feel like it. Since everyone is allowed to be involved in running schools and libraries, the process of running them appears to be simple to other university faculty. This is in contrast to their own fields in most instances. Most individuals do not feel that they can give opinions to the math or physics professor on how to function in their disciplines. The faculty member can rightly feel they are the authority. But, like other members of society, these same authorities in math and physics feel fully qualified to lecture teacher and library educators on their subjects. This creates a definite inferiority view in higher education for library and education schools.

Adding to this problem is that most faculty in higher education learned to teach on their own. They never attended a college of education. They may have never read a book on teaching. Yet, most faculty believe they are good and effective teachers. Hence, they believe that the process of teaching must be easy. After all, even their international teaching assistants with poor English can teach. The knowledge that teacher educators have must not be that important if this reasoning is followed fully. Labaree wrote, "Compounding this resistance to the notion that teachers have special pedagogical skills is the student's general experience that learning is not that hard-and therefore, by extension, that teaching is not hard either."

Librarianship is slightly different. Most faculty have had to use a library. Most have not had to function in library roles. Yet, the perception in higher education is that librarianship is easy academic work. Wrote White, "What faculty members see, or at least what they think they see, does not require a graduate degree in librarianship, although a graduate degree in a 'discipline' might help make the librarians more collegial." Most faculty probably imagine they could be librarians if they wanted to be and that their PHD's ought to qualify them for these roles if they wanted them.

Responses to Academia's Scorn: Not surprisingly, even if attempts at gaining equal recognition on college campuses is futile, teacher and library school faculty have responded to the low status they have on campus. In many cases, this response has manifested itself as an attack on higher education itself. In other instances, it has led library schools to disguise what they do by dropping the word library from their titles. Regardless, few faculty in education or librarianship have acknowledged the validity of the prevailing view in higher education.

There have been some suggestions to respond to this criticism by strengthening the scholarly output of both education and librarianship. There is merit in these arguments. However, even an attempt to increase the amount of high quality theoretical research will not convince most that education or librarianship are valuable academic fields due to other considerations already detailed in this paper. No one in education or librarianship is seriously suggesting that either field should limit the number of women who become practitioners in their field to deal with gender bias in academia.

Many do call for better pay in each field but few expect that this will result in either field being drawn even with other professional fields with better pay. No one can expect that the public will lose its control on schooling or libraries either. Finally, there is no way that higher education faculty can conceivably be made to achieve teacher certification. Hence, the main responses to the low status of education and librarianship in higher education have been reluctant acceptance, an attack on the values of higher education itself and in the case of library schools an attempt to "disguise" the nature of the programmes by dropping the word "library" from their department names.

Wrote Berry, "Maybe it is time to remind the state that it has a responsibility to educate people for public service and that libraries are a fundamental public service. If the university administrators won't hear that message, maybe it is time to take it to the legislatures and governments that support them. By fighting these pernicious academic values we might save our library schools. We might even return our universities to teaching, service and real research." Berry and many library educators see it, the problem is not that librarianship is a low paying profession dominated by women that is engaged in practical matters serving the community. The problem is that higher education does not value public service in low paying, less "prestigious" fields. The solution is to alter the values of higher education and realign the university to its original public service mission.

Stieg shared a similar sentiment. She wrote, "Signs of dissatisfaction with the priorities of the research universities are beginning to appear...If the concept of social responsibilities of universities can be extended to the educational realm, disciplines and programmes less advantaged than law, medicine and business will be helped." This approach by Berry and Stieg not only rebuffs the university for not valuing librarianship (and by extension education) but also holds that the values that these schools hold actually should be emulated by everyone else in the university. This is a bold approach. Recognizing that the values of academia are hopelessly out of line with education and library schools, Berry and Stieg have suggested changing these higher education values because they do not really benefit higher education or the communities that higher education serves.

The Holmes Group, an organization comprising the deans of education of many top ranked education schools, responded to this issue by attacking higher education and those in education schools that emphasized research to the detriment of training new teachers in an attempt to emulate corrupt higher education values. The Holmes Group wrote that "the generally negative attitude in higher education towards matters relating to elementary and secondary education" was corrosive to faculty in education schools. The Holmes Group wants education schools to abandon what it sees as the bad values of higher education such as an emphasis on research. Instead, the Holmes Group wants education schools to dedicate themselves entirely to preparing teachers. In this way, the education school can still function as it was meant to as a professional school without losing itself to what is wrong in higher education.

While Labaree does not agree with much of the Holmes Group report of 1995, he like others echoes the attack on higher education values. Wrote Labaree, "In some ways, ed schools have been doing things right. They have wrestled vigorously with the problems of public education, an area that is of deep concern to most citizens. This has meant tackling social problems of great complexity and practical importance, even though the university does not place much value on the production of this kind of messy, indeterminate and applied knowledge. Oddly enough, the rest of the university could learn a lot from the example of the ed school." Many in education and librarianship agree, the problem is not in education and library schools. The problem is a higher education that does not properly value public service. It is higher education that should change. In reality, faced with scorn and budget/programme cuts, this may be a hard sell in academia. But it may ultimately prove to be the correct response.

Some library schools have tried to fit into the current values of higher education better. They have done this by attempting to hide what they do. Surprisingly, may library schools are dropping the word "library" from their titles. Several schools, including the University of California/Berkley and the University of Michigan have done this. They have replaced their titles with phrases like the School of Information Sciences or the School of Information Science and Technology. The word library does not confer status on campus. However, "information" and "technology" do. Obviously, library schools are schools of information and technology as well. Some library schools hope that by eliminating the word library and replacing it with something more respectable, they will garner more prestige on campus.

This strategy has problems. To begin with, most practicing librarians have responded in anger to the perceived shame that these non-library "library" programmes seem to have in educating librarians. It is not a good idea for a professional school to alienate the members of the profession it serves. And the academy is not fooled by the word change either. Wrote Crowley, "Unfortunately, the march of information loyalists to drive the word 'library' from graduate education will continue. Equally likely, historians and physicists -- if they care and they may not-- will note which department still produces people who work in libraries. The existing views of status will remain and those trying to seize new prestige will be ignored."

However, as bad as the idea may sound, there may be some benefit in changing the names of library schools. Information and technology are part of the library curriculum. Librarians are information managers and web page masters. Asserting the right of the library school to teach these subjects is important. It is time academia realized librarians and libraries are not just about books. Changing the name clearly asserts this. Information management is powerful in higher education now. Therefore, other academic departments such as business and computer science do not want library schools into what they see as their turf. However, why do the library schools feel they have to abandon library from their department name and degree titles? It does not benefit the image of the library profession and it does not really enhance academic status. Everyone still knows that the school is a library school.

Conclusions: Education and library schools have a perception problem on college campuses. The reasons for this are many and varied as has been shown in this paper. No paper can hope to embrace the full scale of this problem. As has been demonstrated, the issues include such matters as gender and class bias, low pay, the nature of the knowledge studied and factors inherent to schools and libraries such as their public nature and that the professions look easy. This paper could not hope to attempt to thoroughly examine all angles and suggest solutions. This paper instead was an attempt to compare the similarities of education and library schools in regards to status.

To the knowledge of this author, this has not been attempted before. Hopefully, this comparison may prove useful to others and some solutions to what seems an unsolvable problem may begin to emerge.

Master of Library and Information Science

Application: The student must apply to both the Graduate School and the School of Information Studies.

Admission: An applicant must meet Graduate School requirements plus the following additional requirements of the School of Information Studies to be considered for admission to the programme:

- Submission of scores on the General Test of the Graduate Record Examination (GRE) or the Miller Analogies Test (MAT). (GRE or MAT scores are currently required of domestic applicants and will be required of international applicants beginning with the summer 2004 admission term.) The test scores should be sent directly to the SOIS. This requirement will be waived for applicants whose overall undergraduate GPA, as calculated by the UWM Graduate School, is at least 3.00, or who already hold another master's degree or Ph.D., or the equivalent.
- Applicants from foreign institutions are required to submit the Test of English as a Foreign Language (TOEFL) score. The minimum acceptable score is 550 PBT, 213 CBT, or 79 IBT. A score of 6.5 or higher on the International English Language Testing System (IELTS) may be submitted in lieu of the TOEFL.
- Two letter of recommendation from persons who can testify to the applicant's likelihood of success in the master's programme in library and information science. References from former teachers or employers are preferred.

No prior coursework in library/information science is required. A student whose undergraduate grade point average is below 2.75 (4.0 basis) may be considered for admission on probation. See the Admission on Probation section of this Bulletin.

Faculty Advisor: Each student is assigned a faculty advisor in the School of Information Studies at the time of admission to the master's programme. The name of the faculty advisor is included in the student's letter of admission and may also be obtained from an academic advisor in the School of Information Studies.

Credits and Courses: The minimum degree requirement is 36 graduate credits, 30 of which must be in library and information science and up to 6 of which may be in related areas. Students who have already completed a master's or doctoral degree in a field other than library science may have the library and information science master's programme reduced to 30 credits. Under special circumstances, up to 6 of these credits may be from another field in a closely allied area with advisor consent. Students who have completed library science courses at the undergraduate level may, upon request, have their coursework reviewed to determine whether the content was the equivalent of that in required courses in the School of Information Studies Programme. However, the establishment of such equivalencies will not reduce the total number of credits required for the master's degree in library and information science, but merely enable the student to avoid unnecessary repetition.

The number of credits needed for each of the coordinated degree programmes is 12 credits less than the sum of credits of the two programmes if taken separately. All degree requirements of each component programme, however, must be satisfied. This includes makeup courses for deficiencies, required courses and graduation proficiency requirements. The MLIS component of each coordinated programme includes 30 credits of SOIS courses including the 15 credits of required courses.

The following are basic required courses:

510 Introduction to Reference Services and Resources, 3 cr.

520 Managing Library Collections, 3 cr.

531 Organization of Information, 3 cr.

540 Management of Libraries and Information Services, 3 cr.

550 Introduction to Information Science, 3 cr.

These courses (or their equivalent) must be completed by full-time students by the end of their second semester; for part-time students, two of the courses must be completed by the end of the second semester and all five by the end of the fifth semester for coursework in the School of Information Studies.

Minimum Grade Requirement in the Basic Required Courses: The minimum grade requirement for 510, 520, 531, 540 and 550 is a B. Students who earn a grade of B- or lower have not met the minimum requirement and will be allowed to repeat the core course once. Students are responsible for tuition in the repeated course. Those who do not meet the minimum grade requirements upon repeating the course will be recommended for academic dismissal. Students may not register for a course for which any of the core courses is a prerequisite until the minimum grade requirement is met.

Proficiency Requirement in Subject

This course of study requires students to demonstrate proficiency in the field of library and information science. There are two options for completing the proficiency requirement: passing a comprehensive examination or completing and successfully defending a thesis.

Comprehensive Examination: Students choosing the comprehensive examination option must successfully pass a written comprehensive examination. A student who fails the examination the first time may repeat it once. However, a student who fails the examination may not select the thesis option.

Thesis Option: Students choosing the thesis option must take at least three credits of thesis coursework in addition to the 36 credits required for the comprehensive examination option, making the minimum credits required for the thesis option 39 credits. However, only 3 credits of thesis coursework may count towards the total degree credit requirement of 39. Those who already have a graduate degree must complete a minimum of 33 credits for this option.

Students who choose the thesis option in the coordinated master's degree programmes also need to take an additional

3 credits of thesis coursework. Thus, while total degree credits vary among the coordinated master's programmes, the Master of Library and Information Science component of each requires 33 credits of SOIS course work, three of which would be taken as thesis credit. Students pursuing thesis options in both programmes will be required to fulfil each programme's thesis requirement and complete two separate theses.

Students in the thesis option also must take a minimum of three credits of research methods. More may be required by individual circumstances, but only the first three credits may count toward degree credit requirements. Either 540-890, Research Methods in Library and Information Science, or a comparable course chosen in consultation with the major professor, can contribute towards satisfaction of this requirement. Students must complete the five core courses in addition to the research methods requirement before defense of the thesis proposal can occur.

Students must register for a variable credit thesis research course L&I Sci 540-898: Master's Thesis (1-3 credits), during every semester of thesis work.

Students may select the thesis option at any point in their course of study, but are encouraged to make this decision and form their thesis committee as early as possible to avoid the necessity of taking additional coursework. The faculty advisor assigned to each student upon admission may serve as the student's thesis advisor, but is not required to do so. It is the student's responsibility to enter into a mutually agreed upon advising relationship with a thesis advisor in SOIS, who then serves as chair of the thesis committee. Likewise, a student may withdraw from the thesis option and pursue the comprehensive examination option; however, the student would need to meet the registration and other requirements for the comprehensive examination set forth in SOIS policies and procedures as published in the SOIS Bulletin.

Students must pass an oral examination in defense of the thesis. The thesis defense may be repeated once.

Time Limit: Students in the 36-credit programme must complete all degree requirements within seven years of initial enrollment. Students in the 30-credit programme must complete all degree requirements within five years of initial enrollment.

Certificate of Advanced Study in Archives and Records Administration: The Certificate of Advanced Study (CAS) in Archives and Records Administration is designed to help working professionals to update their knowledge in core areas of their responsibilities or to develop another specialty in a library-information area. It will enable students to either alter the direction of a career path or to enrich, update and strengthen their skills and their knowledge of their field.

The CAS candidate will complete 15 credits of course work, planned in conjunction with his or her advisor and approved by the Dean of the School of Information Studies as an individually designed programme suited for the needs and professional objectives of the student. A minimum of 12 credits must be taken in the School of Information Studies. Up to 3 credits may be taken in another school or department of the University of Wisconsin-Milwaukee. Students may obtain up to three credits in independent study which is included as a part of the total approved programme.

Certificate of Advanced Study

Attainment of this certificate can be identified as an advanced educational step for individuals who have demonstrated the capabilities and competencies needed by the profession. Such persons can respond to the rapid changes in the field of library and information science through this planned academic programme of specialization.

Admission: Applicant must apply to the Graduate School for admission as a School of Information Studies Non-Degree Candidate and meet these requirements:

- A Master of Library and Information Science degree, or a master's degree in a closely related field such as computer science or educational technology, from an accredited university. Candidates with little or no background in library science will be required to take some courses from the MLIS programme.
- Two letters of recommendation.

- A statement from the applicant which would describe the individual's area of interest and career plan and identify the professional objectives which the applicant would hope to achieve through participation in the Certificate of Advanced Study in Library and Information Science.

Course of Study: The student must complete 15 credits. Courses are planned by the candidate and faculty advisor and approved by the Dean of the School of Information Studies as an individual programme suited for the needs and professional objectives of the student.

- A minimum of 12 of these credits must be taken in the School of Information Studies.
- Up to 3 hours of credit may be taken in another school or department of the University of Wisconsin-Milwaukee.
- A maximum of three graduate credit hours may be transferred from another accredited university provided that the courses are relevant to the candidate's professional objectives and are included as part of the total approved programme.
- No thesis is required, but students may obtain up to three hours of credit in independent research which is included as part of the total approved programme.

A grade point average of 3.0 (B on the scale of 4.0) must be maintained. The programme must be completed within a period of four years from the date of admission.

Library Technicians

Significant Points: Training requirements range from a high school diploma to an associate degree, but computer skills are necessary for all workers. Increasing use of computerized circulation and information systems should continue to spur job growth, but many libraries' budget constraints should moderate growth. Employment should grow rapidly in special libraries because growing numbers of professionals and other workers use those libraries.

Nature of the Work: Library technicians both help librarians acquire, prepare and organize material and assist users in finding information. Library technicians usually work under the supervision of a librarian, although they work independently in certain situations. Technicians in small libraries handle a range of duties; those in large libraries usually specialize. As libraries increasingly use new technologies-such as CD-ROM, the Internet, virtual libraries and automated databases-the duties of library technicians will expand and evolve accordingly. Library technicians are assuming greater responsibilities, in some cases taking on tasks previously performed by librarians.

Depending on the employer, library technicians can have other titles, such as library technical assistant or media aide. Library technicians direct library users to standard references, organize and maintain periodicals, prepare volumes for binding, handle interlibrary loan requests, prepare invoices, perform routine cataloguing and coding of library materials, retrieve information from computer databases and supervise support staff.

The widespread use of computerized information storage and retrieval systems has resulted in technicians handling technical services-such as entering catalogue information into the library's computer-that were once performed by librarians. Technicians assist with customizing databases. In addition, technicians instruct patrons in how to use computer systems to access data. The increased automation of record-keeping has reduced the amount of clerical work performed by library technicians. Many libraries now offer self-service registration and circulation areas with computers, decreasing the time library technicians spend manually recording and inputting records.

Some library technicians operate and maintain audiovisual equipment, such as projectors, tape and CD players and DVD and videocassette players and assist users with microfilm or microfiche readers. They also design posters, bulletin boards, or displays.

Library technicians in school libraries encourage and teach students to use the library and media center. They also help teachers obtain instructional materials and they assist students with special assignments. Some work in special libraries maintained by government agencies, corporations, law firms, advertising agencies, museums, professional societies, medical centres and research laboratories, where they conduct literature searches, compile bibliographies and prepare abstracts, usually on subjects of particular interest to the organization.

To extend library services to more patrons, many libraries operate bookmobiles, often run by library technicians. The technicians take trucks stocked with books, or bookmobiles, to designated sites on a regular schedule, frequently stopping at shopping centres, apartment complexes, schools and nursing homes. Bookmobiles also may be used to extend library service to patrons living in remote areas. Depending on local conditions, the technicians may operate a bookmobile alone or may be accompanied by another library employee.

Library technicians who drive bookmobiles are responsible for answering patrons' questions, receiving and checking out books, collecting fines, maintaining the book collection, shelving materials and occasionally operating audiovisual equipment to show slides or films. They participate and may assist, in planning programmes sponsored by the library, such as reader advisory programmes, used-book sales, or outreach programmes. Technicians who drive the bookmobile keep track of their mileage, the materials lent out and the amount of fines collected. In some areas, they are responsible for maintenance of the vehicle and any photocopiers or other equipment in it. They record statistics on circulation and the number of people visiting the bookmobile. Technicians also may record requests for special items from the main library and arrange for the materials to be mailed or delivered to a patron during the next scheduled visit. Many bookmobiles are equipped with personal computers and CD-ROM systems linked to the main library system, allowing technicians to reserve or locate books immediately. Some bookmobiles now offer Internet access to users.

Working Conditions: Technicians answer questions and provide assistance to library users. Those who prepare library materials sit at desks or computer terminals for long periods and can develop headaches or eyestrain from working with the terminals. Some duties, like calculating circulation statistics, can be repetitive and boring. Others, such as performing computer searches with the use of local and regional library networks and cooperatives, can be interesting and challenging. Library technicians may lift and carry books, climb ladders to reach high stacks and bend low to shelve books on bottom shelves.

Library technicians in school libraries work regular school hours. Those in public libraries and college and university (academic) libraries also work weekends, evenings and some holidays. Library technicians in special libraries usually work normal business hours, although they often work overtime as well.

The schedules of library technicians who drive bookmobiles depend on the size of the area being served. Some bookmobiles operate every day, while others go only on certain days. Some bookmobiles operate in the evenings and weekends, to give patrons as much access to the library as possible. Because library technicians who operate bookmobiles may be the only link some people have to the library, much of their work consists of helping the public. They may assist handicapped or elderly patrons to the bookmobile or shovel snow to ensure their safety. They may enter hospitals or nursing homes to deliver books to patrons who are bedridden.

Training, Other Qualifications and Advancement: Training requirements for library technicians vary widely, ranging from a high school diploma to specialized post-secondary training. Some employers hire individuals with work experience or other training; others train inexperienced workers on the job. Many employers prefer to hire technicians who have an associate degree or some other post-secondary training. Given the rapid spread of automation in libraries, computer skills are a necessity, with knowledge of databases, library automation systems, online library systems, online public access systems and circulation systems particularly valuable. Many bookmobile drivers are required to have a commercial driver's license.

Some community colleges offer an associate degree or certificate programmes designed for library technicians.

Programmes include both liberal arts and library-related study. Students learn about library and media organization and operation, as well as how to order, process, catalogue, locate and circulate library materials and work with library automation. Libraries and associations offer continuing education courses to keep technicians abreast of new developments in the field.

Library technicians usually advance by assuming added responsibilities. For example, technicians often start at the circulation desk, checking books in and out. After gaining experience, they may become responsible for storing and verifying information. As they advance, they may become involved in budget and personnel matters in their departments. Some library technicians advance to supervisory positions and are in charge of the day-to-day operation of their departments.

Employment: Library technicians held about 122,000 jobs in 2004; almost half worked in county or municipal public libraries. Most of the rest worked in school or academic libraries, while some worked in special libraries for health and legal services. The Federal Government employs library technicians primarily at the US Department of Defense and the US Library of Congress.

Job Outlook: Employment of library technicians is expected to grow about as fast as the average for all occupations through 2014. In addition to jobs opening up through employment growth, some job openings will result from the need to replace library technicians who transfer to other fields or leave the labour force.

The increasing use of library automation is expected to continue to spur job growth among library technicians. Computerized information systems have simplified certain tasks, such as descriptive cataloguing, which can now be handled by technicians instead of librarians. For example, technicians now can easily retrieve information from a central database and store it in the library's computer. Although efforts to contain costs could dampen employment growth of library technicians in school, public and college and university libraries, cost containment efforts could also result in hiring more library technicians than librarians. Growth in the number of professionals and other workers who use special libraries should result in good job opportunities for library technicians in those settings.

Earnings: Median annual earnings of library technicians in May 2004 were $24,940. The middle 50 percent earned between $18,640 and $32,600. The lowest 10 percent earned less than $14,760 and the highest 10 percent earned more than $40,730. Median annual earnings in the industries employing the largest numbers of library technicians in May 2004 were as follows:

Colleges, universities and professional schools	$28,940
Local government	23,560
Other information services	22,550
Elementary and secondary schools	22,510

Salaries of library technicians in the Federal Government averaged $39,647 in 2005.

Transferring Library Technician Skills

Global Work Environments: 'In Australia, we work in a global environment that has been transfigured by the introduction of telecommunications, broadcasting and computing technologies which impact on both our working and personal lives. This is causing social and economic readjustments, which sees declining workforce numbers in mining, manufacturing and farming and dramatic reorganisation in government departments at national, state and local levels'. (Reid 1997 p152)

The changes we are experiencing are still relatively new, with the pace over the last forty years being equivalent to complete eras. In the 1980s, when the global marketplace arrived in Australia in the form of competition and economic rationalism, organisations were faced with the need to rethink the way they did business. As a result 'between 1993 and 1995, 56 percent of larger Australian organisations downsized and in 1997-98, more than sixty-two per cent of all-sized organisations took this path.' Johnston (2000).

Ultimately what these streamlined businesses now demand is a workforce that is flexible enough to respond to increasingly shifting patterns of employment. The concept of the secure, full-time job is under threat from part-time, contract and temporary workforces who are asked to adapt to and provide the range of skills that the industry is seeking. Pressure is placed on the employee to offer employers continual skills development and an ability to adapt to required needs, which may, or may not be, related to their core training.

An OECD report: Technology, Productivity and Job Creation (OECD 1996) highlights the shift in organisational models with the emphasis being on core groups of employees with high skill levels who take central roles in managing the organization and draw on expertise as required for particular projects in the form of contract workers, consultants, temporary staff and outworkers. As an indication of changing work practices the following chart provides a historical breakdown of key characteristics of the Industrial and Information ages:

Economic Characteristics	
Industrial period	*Information Period*
Centralised workplace	Distributed workplaces
Economies of scale	Flexibility of scale and place
Organisational characteristics	
Labour contract	Temporary agreements
Rationalised division of labour	Partial reintegrated labour
Close supervision	Individual/group responsibility
Hierarchy (later bureaucracy)	Flatter structure
Vertical integration	Horizontal integration
Technical Characteristics	
Mechanisation (later automation)	Communication
Product based	Information based
Sequential flow	Distribution

Impact of Technology on the Library

The impact of technology on libraries is not limited to Australia and although the literature search concentrated on Australian material, information that reflects the situation elsewhere has been incorporated.

At the 10th National Library Technician's Conference in 1999 the opinion was (Grant 1999) that libraries today are facing change at a pace that is unprecedented in history. The reasons for change at such a pace? Grânt claims that it is technology that is the 'driving force'. Consider some of the ways that technology has been introduced into libraries to 'support' the delivery of services and resources to ever increasing and diversified client bases:

- Digitisation;
- E-journals and e-books;
- E-reserve;
- Computer-based learning platforms;
- The web;
- E-commerce;
- Metadata;
- Synchronous communication tools - offering real-time reference support via computer and modem;
- Community networks.

With many of these initiatives there has been a need to collaborate with a wider range of information professionals, particularly those with IT knowledge. Is it possible that this could lead to a decreasing need for library-trained staff and an increased need for hybrid workers? It is interesting to note that selected graduate library and information courses are shifting the focus of their courses from specific library based skills to structure that represents the teaching of information management in all its aspects. Whether or not this is a correct approach is not under consideration here, but is used simply to reflect the changing view of 'information supply and management'.

'Technology remains one of the primary drivers of change in the ways that people work, seek information, communication and entertain themselves. For the library, there is a stronger emphasis on content, context, customer service, training and collaboration with information technology staff. ' (Drake 2000)

As Saurine (2000) observes 'there is no question that new technologies and the Internet are the factor that have challenged traditional library services and practices.'

In fact it has been stated that computers have made the most impact on libraries in areas that require 'the rapid and accurate storage and processing of structured data, the ability to operate for 24 hours a day, seven days a week and world wide connectivity and communication.' (Dunsire 2001) The impact this has on staffing is of particular relevance to paraprofessionals, with Dunsire claiming that the application of this technology reduces the need for many of the specialist clerical type skills that have traditionally been performed by library technicians .....'and it is not difficult to imagine an effective library service without paraprofessional staff. Many American libraries use volunteer lay persons for this type of work'

Supporting this, Evans (2000) identifies key areas of 'recording stock (cataloguing) and its movement (circulation)' as those most affected by technological change. Continuing the discussion, Evans states that the next step is that of 'seamless interlending of material, utilising the strengths of developing standards and faster and more efficient technologies'. One indication of this is LIDDAS, an international consortia development, of which Macquarie University Library is a member. LIDDAS aims at creating user-controlled access to the interlending and document delivery process. Combine this with online journal access and it is not unreasonable to perceive reduced requirements for paraprofessionals within these previously key areas.

What does this all mean for library technicians in the future? Martyn (1997 p225) asks 'how many library workers, in the last decade, have experienced one or more of the following organisational change processes: down-sizing, restructuring, outsourcing, re-engineering, centralisation, decentralisation, amalgamation, computerisation, or, personally been upgraded, downgraded, re-trained, retrenched or reclassified?' In her study Martyn identified technology, along with budget constraints, outsourcing and commercialisation of services as major factor in the shifting workplace environment.

This is further highlighted in Debowski's (1999) consideration of key influences:

1. Significant advances in technology and increasing costs

of journals and other print resources—massive growth in electronic services

2. Budgetary manoeuvres—staffing pared down to essential levels so that infrastructure services may be developed
3. Decreasing numbers of library visitors. Reduced coverage of service points, sustaining basic services whilst offering extended electronic access
4. Outsourcing—argument for a more cost effective system

The risk to libraries may lie in not recognising fully the impact of the global market and the role of libraries within this marketplace. The way is being left open for 'new players' to undertake the role of information provision. It is possible to see this type of change in the increasing use of information brokers, news services and the public use of the Internet as an information source. (Hobohm 1996)

Whilst these views may be seen as alarming and/or challenging, they should also be seen as an opportunity, for there is a corresponding availability of diverse roles that have evolved from and in response to new technologies. These roles incorporate those such as - Internet search expert; Webmaster; Web site designer and Intranet developer. Whilst not specifically administrative or technical they require a flexible mindset with an emphasis on attitudes, aptitudes and approaches.. in short an ability to transfer previous learning to new responsibilities and environments offering key results and outcomes for employers. Interestingly and relevant to this point, Sciacca (1993) noted that it was often library technicians who are first to be confronted with, adapt to and quickly acquire new skills in relation to new technology within the library.

The alternate viewpoints about the future of libraries and the career potential for library staff are not the focus here. The evidence that technology has had a major impact on libraries is obvious, particularly in relation to staffing levels and key responsibilities. Hyde, (1997) suggests that in the future, staff will work, not in a physical library, but elsewhere with all electronic access to collections. Where there is a need for a physical location for those resources, print and otherwise that are not available or required in an electronic form, he predicts possible management options includes the increased outsourcing of major functions. This would prove to be particularly relevant to the cataloguing and current awareness service areas where there are currently large numbers of library technicians involved. In response to these demands library technicians need to be able to adapt quickly, develop the new skills that are required and be flexible in their career expectations. This outlook will support the change process whilst also creating personal and professional opportunities to reshape and redefine their future.

Survey of Library Technicians

Stage two of this research project involved the development of a survey based on information obtained in the literature review. Library technicians were chosen as the sample group for the survey. The aim of the survey was to determine how current, accurate and useful job descriptions are in Australian libraries.

Methodology: Surveys were sent to library technicians in all states within Australia, the Northern Territory and Australian Capitol Territory and represented special, public, academic and school libraries. A total of 303 surveys were distributed. Names of survey participants were identified from the delegates' list of the 9th National Library Technicians Conference held in 1997. Additional surveys were sent to willing participants identified through the Library Technician Discussion Group, LibTec. A maximum of three surveys was sent to each library, in order to gain as broad a representation of libraries as possible.

Participants were asked to complete the survey whether they did or did not have a job description. They were also asked to include a copy of their current job description if possible. A prize of $100 was offered to participants as an incentive to return their survey and to improve the response rate. Participants were given approximately one month to return the surveys. The first three questions of the survey obtained background information regarding library technician status, experience in libraries and the type of library. Other questions in the survey focussed on the accuracy, updating, reviewing, uses and content of job descriptions. A copy of the survey is in appendix.

Results: 200 surveys were returned including four surveys that were not completed because the respondents were educators rather than library technicians. This represents a 66 percent response rate. This is an excellent response rate as a statistical consulting firm indicated any response rate over 30 percent was a good result. The winner of the $100 was Bruce Lowth from Palmerston Library. Approximately 67 percent of respondents included a copy of their job descriptions, which provided valuable additional content information that is incorporated into the results. The majority of respondents (83 percent) had completed a Library Technician qualification. 60 percent had more than ten years experience in libraries; 27 percent had 6-10 years; 12 percent had 2-5 years and 2 percent had 0-1 years.

The type of libraries represented in the survey are shown in Figure:

- Academic Libraries- 81 surveys - 41 percent
- Public Libraries- 34 surveys -17 percent
- Special Libraries- 61 surveys - 31 percent
- School Libraries- 15 surveys - 8 percent
- Other libraries - 5 surveys - 3 percent

Surveys were returned from all states within Australia, the Northern Territory and Australian Capital Territory.

Type of Libraries Represented in the Survey

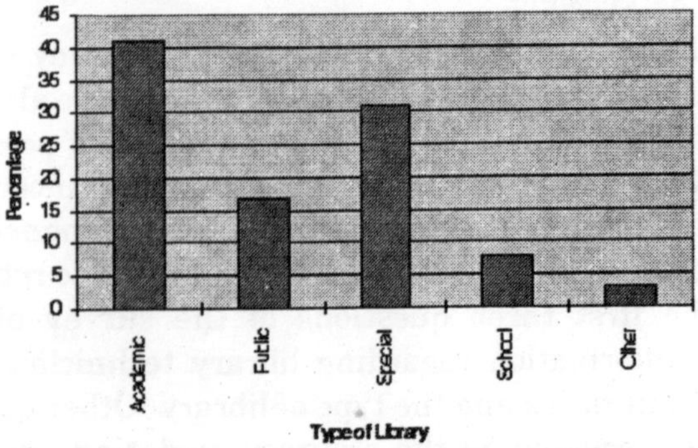

An overwhelming majority of respondents (93 percent) had job descriptions for their current position. Of these, 27 percent felt that their job description was very accurate; 46 percent felt they were mostly accurate; 22 percent felt they were somewhat accurate and 5 percent felt they were not accurate at all.

In relation to the updating of job descriptions, 24 percent had been updated in the last six months; 19 percent had been updated in the last 6 to 12 months; 23 percent had been updated in the last one to two years and 34 percent had not been updated for over two years.

Figure illustrates when job descriptions are reviewed or updated. The main reasons for reviewing a job description are when a job becomes vacant (45 percent) or when a job is reclassified (30 percent). Only 15 percent of respondents reviewed jobs annually.

When Job Descriptions are Reviewed

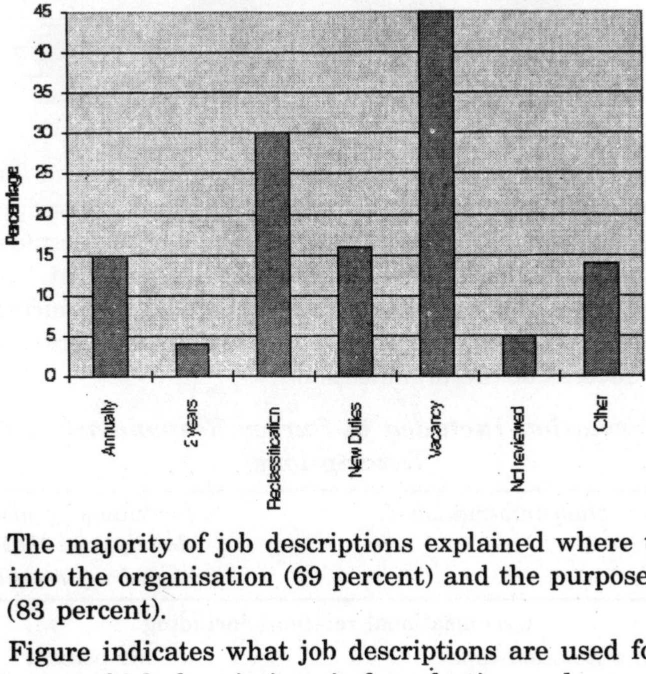

The majority of job descriptions explained where the job fits into the organisation (69 percent) and the purpose of the job (83 percent).

Figure indicates what job descriptions are used for. The main use of job descriptions is for selection and recruitment

(74 percent). 55 percent used them in performance appraisals. 18 percent used them to identify training needs and 16 percent used them in the induction process. For the majority of respondents performance standards (78 percent), time or percentages for each duty (86 percent) and goals, mission, vision or outputs (55 percent) are NOT included in job descriptions. 45 percent of respondents indicated that their library had a separate person/job specification; 32 percent said they did not and 23 percent were unsure. A summary sheet indicating the number of responses for each question is in appendix.

Uses of job Descriptions

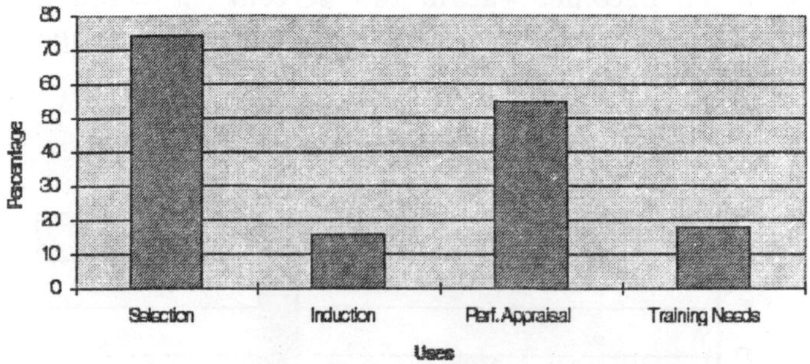

Figure illustrates the type of information included in job descriptions returned with the survey. These job descriptions ranged from half a page, which did not describe the purpose of the job or where it fitted into the organisation, to job descriptions that were four and five pages in length which gave a detailed overview of the job, how it fitted into and contributed to the success of the organisation.

Information Included in Survey Respondents Job Descriptions

Job description information	*Percentage of job descriptions that included information*
Organisational relations including	
Reporting Relationships	64 percent
Duties/tasks	59 percent

Contd...

Job Description information	*Percentage of job descriptions that included information*
Job function/purpose	53 percent
Education/Qualifications/Knowledge	44 percent
Skills	36 percent
Responsibilities	33 percent
Experience	31 percent
Environment	25 percent
Selection criteria	21 percent
Accountabilities	20 percent
Authority	20 percent
Contacts	12 percent
Performance Standards	9 percent
Challenges	9 percent
Time/percentages/Frequency	9 percent

Comparison with Survey Conducted by the Association of Research Libraries: The Association of Research Libraries (ARL) conducted a survey of librarian job descriptions in 1993 (Ray and Hawthorne, 1993). The aim of this survey was to capture background information on the currency, content and use of librarian job descriptions. Figure compares survey questions that were directly comparable between this survey and the library technician survey.

Comparison between ARL Survey and Library Technician Survey

Survey Information	*Percent Result from ARL (1993) Survey*	*Percent result from Library Technician Survey*
	Accuracy of job description	
Very accurate	29 percent	27 percent
Mostly accurate	56 percent	46 percent
Somewhat accurate	15 percent	22 percent
	When job descriptions are reviewed?	
Annually	35 percent	15 percent
	Uses of job descriptions	

Contd..

Survey Information	*Percent Result from ARL (1993) Survey*	*Percent result from Library Technician Survey*
Selection and recruitment	85 percent	74 percent
Performance Appraisals	75 percent	55 percent
Identifying Training Needs	60 percent	18 percent
	Describe the purpose of the job	
Yes	89 percent	83 percent
No	11 percent	17 percent
	Are time/percentages used?	
Yes	25 percent	14 percent
No	75 percent	86 percent
	Are performance standards included?	
Yes	6 percent	22 percent
No	92 percent	78 percent

Although the ARL survey was conducted five-six years ago it is interesting to note the comparison in results. The ARL survey indicates that respondents found their job descriptions to be more accurate. The reason for this may be due to the larger percentage of libraries reviewing job descriptions annually and using them in performance appraisals. It is also evident from this comparison that Australian libraries are beginning to incorporate performance standards into their job descriptions although this only represents a small percentage.

Findings: As the response rate from this survey was over 30 percent and represented academic, special, public and school libraries the following findings may be generalised to the library industry.

- Job descriptions are developed and used by the majority of libraries and employees feel that they are mostly accurate (46 percent). This is not surprising considering firstly that the majority of job descriptions had not been reviewed for over two years and secondly the constantly changing library environment.
- The greater number of libraries represented do not have a mechanism to regularly review job descriptions as the majority of job descriptions (34 percent) had not been

reviewed in the last two years. Job descriptions are most commonly reviewed when a job becomes vacant or is reclassified.

- Selection and recruitment appear to be the main purpose for which job descriptions are used in libraries. 55 percent of respondents indicated that they were used in performance appraisals, however, it is unclear if they are reviewed in this process. Job descriptions are not often used for identifying training needs or in the induction process.
- The majority of library job descriptions do describe the purpose of the job and where the job fits into the organisation, although it is unclear how detailed this is as the majority do not indicate the goals, mission or vision of the organisation. For the question - Does your job description explain where your job fits into the organisation, it appears from the sample descriptions that it is mainly described through an organisational chart.
- Time or percentages are rarely included in job descriptions (14 percent). Examples of descriptions that include percentages seem to be those that focus on duties rather than major responsibilities. Performance standards for the majority of libraries are also not included, although many include accountabilities.

Additional comments made by respondents indicate that the question regarding whether libraries have a separate person/ job specification caused confusion and many respondents were unsure about what I meant.

The aim of this questions was to determine whether details about the person's attributes or qualifications required to do the job were included in the same document as the job description or separately. For this reason it is difficult to generalise findings for this area. From the job descriptions returned with the surveys, some libraries label job specifications and person specifications separately while other libraries include both types of information in their job descriptions but do not label them.

Accountabilities in the literature refers to the results expected, however, when analysing the library job descriptions accountabilities were often a list of responsibilities or who the position was accountable to, very few outlined the results expected. Some libraries are beginning to use job descriptions as a performance management tool as they include performance measures or standards, although this is still only a small percentage (22 percent). Performance measures identified were both qualitative - 'polite, courteous and efficient client service' and quantitative in nature - 'number of complaints received each quarter'. Some job descriptions did not identify the standards but outlined that there was an expectation that they would be developed as part of the job - 'Performance standards will be negotiated between the incumbent and the Manger Library Services as part of the ongoing performance management programme.' (Please note: these examples were taken from examples of job descriptions returned with the survey).

Some job descriptions included the selection criteria for the job in the job description and this is usually split into essential and desirable. This aids the library in using the job description as a tool in selection and recruitment as the criteria are clearly labelled for advertising, culling and interviewing applicants.

Survey of Organisations

In my initial proposal for the scholarship, the aim of this stage of the research was to survey organisations that were considered best practice in the design and implementation of job descriptions. This proved a difficult task, as the available literature did not specify organisations that excelled in this area. However, the HR Best Practices in Australasian Companies: 1997 Report did specify organisations that were considered best practice in human resource management.

The aim of this survey was to determine the following aspects of job descriptions within organisations other than libraries.

- When were job descriptions reviewed?
- What were job descriptions used for within the organisation?

- Were performance standards included in the job description?

Methodology: Surveys were sent to organisations identified in the HR Best Practices in Australasian Companies: 1997 Report. As this resulted in a small number of organisations, additional surveys were sent to organisations that had been awarded the Australian Quality Award; Investors in People or were recommended to me for their usage and content of job descriptions. A wide range of organisations were included in the survey, for example, banks, councils, hotels, airlines, food production companies and manufacturing industry.

The survey also asked organisations to include a copy of their job description when they returned the survey. A reply paid address envelope was included with the survey.

Results: A total of 30 surveys were distributed. Seventeen were returned which represents a 57 percent response rate. Appendix 6 outlines a summary of results.

All respondents to the organisation survey used job descriptions within their organisations.

Figure illustrates when job descriptions are reviewed or updated. Results indicate that the main reasons for reviewing a job description are when a job becomes vacant (82 percent) or when a job is reclassified (59 percent). 29 percent of respondents reviewed jobs annually.

When Job Descriptions are Reviewed—Organisation Survey

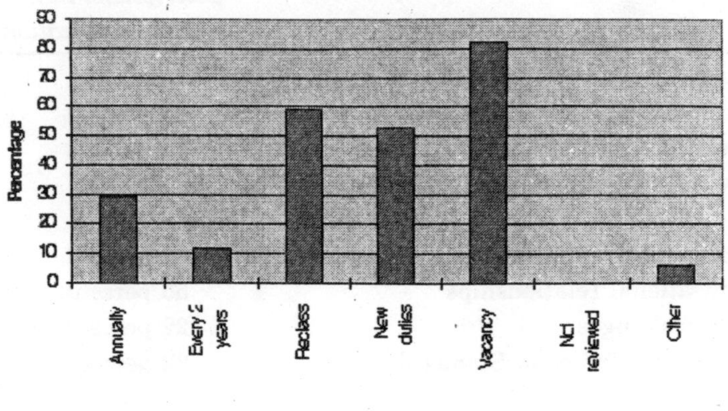

Figure indicates the uses of job descriptions. The main use of job descriptions is for selection and recruitment (100 percent). A large percentage (77 percent) also incorporated job descriptions into their performance appraisal system.

Uses of Job Descriptions—Organisation Survey

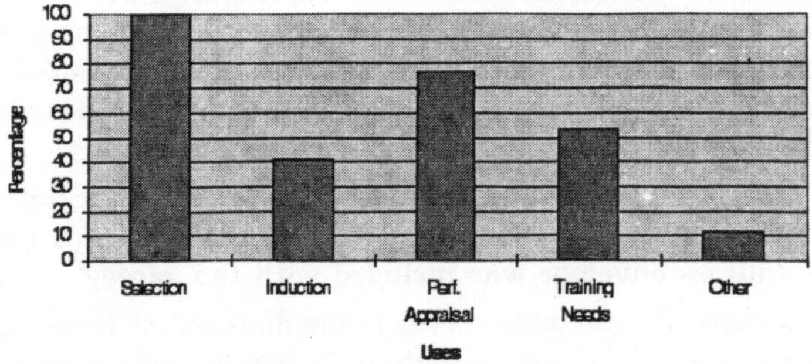

47 percent of respondents included performance standards in their job descriptions.

Nine respondents (53 percent) included a copy of their organisation's job description.

Figure illustrates the type of information included in job descriptions returned with the organisation surveys.

Information Included in Organisation Survey Respondents Job Descriptions

Job description information	*Percentage of job descriptions that included information*
Purpose of position/Objectives	
Responsibility Areas/Key Result	89 percent
Areas/Key Accountabilities	78 percent
Knowledge/Qualifications/Experience	
Working Relationships/Reporting	
relationships, including	66 percent
organisational relationships	55 percent
Major challenges	22 percent
Performance Indicator/Standard	22 percent

Contd...

Job description information	*Percentage of job descriptions that included information*
Authority/Decision Making	11 percent
Position Size Dimensions	11 percent
Delegations	11 percent
Corporate goals	11 percent

Findings: Comparison of the results from the library technician survey and organisation survey is shown in Figure. These results indicate that organisations identified for their quality human resource practices make more extensive use of job descriptions within their organisations (especially in the areas of identifying training needs and performance appraisal) and review them more frequently. Results also indicate that more organisations (47 percent) are incorporating performance standards into their job descriptions than libraries (22 percent).

Comparison of Results from Library Technician Survey and Organisational Survey

Question	*percent result from Library Technician Survey*	*percent result from survey of other organisations*
When are job descriptions reviewed in your organisation?		
Annually	*15 percent*	*29 percent*
Every two years	*4 percent*	*12 percent*
When jobs are reclassified	*30 percent*	*59 percent*
When new duties are added	*16 percent*	*53 percent*
When a job becomes vacant	*45 percent*	*82 percent*
Not reviewed	*5 percent*	*0 percent*
Other	*14 percent*	*6 percent*
What are job descriptions used for in your organisation?		
Selection and recruitment	*74 percent*	*100 percent*
Induction / Orientation	*16 percent*	*41 percent*

Contd...

Question	*percent result from Library Technician Survey*	*percent result from survey of other organisations*
	Performance	
Appraisals / Reviews	*55 percent*	*77 percent*
Identifying Training Needs	*18 percent*	*53 percent*
Other	*0 percent*	*12 percent*
Are performance standards included in the job description?		
Yes	*22 percent*	*47 percent*
No	*78 percent*	*53 percent*

Discussion: From the findings of the Library Technician survey and the information contained in job descriptions returned with the survey it appears that many libraries are using outdated job descriptions that do not meet the needs of today's work environment. They focus on what a person is required to do, that is their duties, rather than on what the person is expected to achieve, that is major responsibilities and outcomes. It is interesting to note, in comparison, that the organisation job description examples (returned with the survey) focussed on responsibilities or key result areas rather than duties.

I found it interesting that the vast majority of descriptions (from both the library technician survey and the organisation survey) did not include the mission statement of the organisation, goals or an explanation of how the job fits into the overall objectives of the department, team or organisation. Again this information is important if the job description is to reflect the interdependence of the job within the organisation and how it contributes to the overall success of the organisation. Absence of this information makes the job description very individual in nature and makes it appear that the job is conducted in isolation. This encourages independent rather than team action (Dunn, 1993).

As mentioned in the literature, job descriptions are a useful tool that can be used for many human resource functions. Some libraries are using their job descriptions to serve several purposes. For example: The Australian Courts and Administration Authority Library states that their Job and Person Specifications serve the following functions:

- when filling a vacant position, to provide both job applicants and the selection panel with information on the responsibilities and duties of a job and the skills and knowledge that it requires; and assist in ensuring selection based on merit
- to assist with induction and training
- when reviewing an employee's performance, to provide a basis for discussion
- when considering and refining organisational goals, to provide information on the relationship of the position to others within the organisation and to the organisation's function
- when considering job classification, to provide base information on the responsibilities and reporting relationships associated with the position

However this library appears to be in the minority, as findings suggest that libraries mainly use job descriptions as [illegible] and recruitment tool. In comparison, when examining the results of the organisation survey it is clear that many organisations are making extensive use of their job descriptions and using them for a variety of purposes.

The inclusion of performance standards in job descriptions is one area that libraries need to explore in the future. They allow the organisation to communicate expectations to the employee especially if the organisation has identified or articulated performance indicators or service standards. Results from the organisation survey suggest that organisations are moving in this direction and using job descriptions as a performance management tool.

Some organisations have moved to providing generic job descriptions for employees performing similar responsibilities. Jones (1996) argues that generic job descriptions provide flexibility because they address expectations and accountabilities rather than the details of how a task should be performed. While there has been a shift to focus on expectations and end results, I believe that generic job descriptions are not as effective as individual job descriptions as they do not encourage ownership or commitment and fail to demonstrate to the employee that their job, responsibilities and contribution are valued by the organisation. While many jobs are similar there may be one or two different areas of responsibility for a particular job.

Where Competencies Fit?

Competencies are 'all the knowledge, skills and attitudes people use in order to fulfil their mission in the company' (Devisch, 1998). As the Library Industry Competency Standards (1995, p.3) 'reflect performance requirements' and adopt an outside-in approach to jobs they are a very useful tool to provide input into the development of job descriptions. Competencies are helpful in identifying the qualities of the person required to perform the job. They can also provide information on responsibility areas and examples of performance indicators or measures, however, it is important to tailor job descriptions to meet the needs of the individual organisation. It is also important to focus on the key competencies required for a position as the job description is meant to provide an overview of the position and identify major responsibilities.

Some organisations have identified core competencies which relate to their organisational values and these are often included or reflected in the job description. In addition some organisations have developed Competency Profiles for each position within their organisation, for example, Murdoch Magazines. These profiles outline key organisational competencies, key management competencies and key functional (technical) competencies. The profiles are incorporated into the organisations performance management system and form the basis for job profiles, recruitment guides, performance assessments and career/development programmes.

Recommendations: As Ray and Hawthorne, (1993. p.i) state 'maintaining a current job description in today's environment of rapid technological change and increased demand for professional and managerial flexibility represents a challenge for both libraries and librarians'. The following recommendations are based on the research and surveys conducted as part of this project. I believe that if libraries adopted these recommendations their job descriptions would be current, accurate and could be used for a variety of purposes.

1. Before developing job descriptions, the library first needs to determine what they will be used for. This will then provide information on what content is to be included. I believe that if organisations are going to invest the time and effort into developing job descriptions they should be used for more than selection and recruitment. As discussed in this paper their uses extend far beyond this, for example, identifying training needs, induction, performance management and career development. The success in writing and using job descriptions depend on this critical first step (Degner, 1995).
2. Libraries need to focus on specific rather than generic job descriptions. This encourages ownership of the job and helps the library to determine that all responsibilities within the library are performed. It also lets employees know that their contributions to the library are individually valued.
3. When writing a job description it should be kept in mind that the job is described in enough detail so that the reader can understand:
    - how the job fits into and contributes to the organisation
    - the purpose of the job
    - major responsibilities of the job
    - the work standards which apply to the job
    - the skills, experience and education required to perform the job.
4. The main output that the majority of libraries produce is service, service to our clients (whether they be internal or external clients). I found it surprising that many of the job descriptions included with the library technician survey did not reflect the importance of client service. I

believe library job descriptions need to be client focused and service orientated in order to accurately reflect the nature of our work.

5. The most important recommendation, from this research, is that job descriptions are aligned with an organisation's management framework and are representative of this framework. For example, the job description needs to reflect the organisation's culture by incorporating its mission statement, performance indicators, critical success factors, values or goals. This provides potential employees information on the culture of the organisation and outlines what is expected of them by the organisation.

While the format, writing style, content and details of job descriptions vary tremendously from library to library the following elements (although different headings may be used) are recommended for inclusion in job descriptions in order to improve their accuracy, currency and usefulness.

- Overview of the organisation—the job description needs to provide a clear and realistic overview of not only the job but also the organisation. As this research indicates that the majority of libraries use job descriptions in selection and recruitment it is important that the description provides an overview of the organisation.
- Purpose of the job—this statement should explain the reason why the job is necessary and show the way the job contributes to organisational goals. For example - To fulfil the mission of... (Cervenka, 1997)
- How the job fits into the library—this needs to be addressed in more detail than the inclusion of an organisational chart. An overview of both the organisation and team/department environment should be included. For example if the job is part of a team then this should be emphasised. This approach will avoid the job description appearing individualistic in nature and illustrate the interdependence of today's work environment.
- Reporting relationships—including who the person reports to and who the position supervises.

- Major responsibilities—the job description should focus on responsibilities and outcomes rather than a detailed list of tasks or duties. It is important that the responsibilities relate to organisational goals or objectives. This helps link the job to the organisation rather than viewing it in isolation.
- Challenges—this section lists the principal challenges or problems faced by the employee in achieving the results of the position. These may be related to job complexity, economic and environmental aspects or growth potential. Again this communicates to the employee what is expected in the position.
- Results expected/ performance indicators/expected results/ key outcomes—these should relate to the library's service standards or performance indicators rather than to individual performance, for example, meet cataloguing service standard rather than catalogues ten books per day. If performance indicators are to be developed as part of a performance management system then this should be stated in the description.
- Qualifications, Experience and Skills—this section includes qualifications and experience required for the position plus all the practical, functional and technical skills. Identification of these as essential or desirable will aid in developing selection criteria for a position.
- Attributes or Behavioural competencies—this section identifies any individual, interpersonal and/or managerial competencies or qualities that an employee needs to possess (*e.g.*: flexibility, stress tolerance, teamwork, planning etc.) Where possible these should be related to the organisational culture, values or identified core competencies.

Other recommendations include.

- Job descriptions are written in conjunction with the person currently doing the job as they are in the best position to know what the job involves. Input can also be gained from the manager and team members. Staff input encourages ownership and accountability and motivates the employee's full commitment. When writing the job description we need to focus on the end results and use an outside-in perspective rather than an inside-out perspective and this needs to be communicated to all staff.

- The format of the job description be clearly set out and easy to read. While some job descriptions include valuable information, they may be hard and time consuming to understand because of their format. The format can be improved through the use of holding information to make sections stand out or with the use of columns and tables.
- Job descriptions do give some direction to employees, however, it should be remembered that job descriptions are only one aspect of human resource management and are used in conjunction with other systems, tools and documents. Libraries need to avoid trying to include too much information in the job description.
- Employees have access to their own job description. If job descriptions are used for career planning, all employees should have access to the job descriptions for all positions within the library. Some organisations have made this possible by placing all job descriptions for their organisations of their Intranet.
- Job descriptions are promoted to employees of the library as a 'overview' of major responsibilities and expectations, not an all-encompassing list of expected tasks and duties. Some libraries have used the word job or position profile rather than description as this suggests an outline or overview of a job rather than a statement describing the job.
- Job descriptions must be reviewed regularly to ensure they remain consistent with the goals and objectives of the organisation (Cervenka, 1997), this may be incorporated into a performance management system. Regular review also allows employees to have a clear understanding of responsibilities and expectations. As Degner (1995) explains, the job description process is continual, it is not a one off event.

- It is important to have an adequate and comprehensive communication programme in place when establishing or revising a job description programme (How to write job descriptions the easy way, 1993). Employees need to be kept informed of what the organisation is doing and why.
- Job descriptions need to be standardised across the organisation.

Appendix 7 includes an example of a job description that incorporates many of the above recommendations. The first section of the Position and Person Profile provides an overview of the position and the role the position plays within the organisation. This overview also illustrates the interdependent nature of the position by providing a summary of the organisational environment (including organisational culture), organisational structure and team environment (including team goals and key processes). The aim of this overview is also to communicate organisational expectations to an employee or prospective employee.

The Person Profile outlines the qualifications, experience, skills and personal attributes of the person required to perform the job. The skills are linked to the organisations identified core competencies and the personal attributes are linked the organisations identified Values. The Position Profile outlines the major responsibilities of the position which are linked to the organisations identified Critical Success Factors. The performance outcomes highlight the end results expected from the major responsibilities while the performance indicators are measures of accomplishment for each responsibility. These indicators are largely linked to organisation or team service standards and performance indicators rather than individual performance indicators in order to illustrate the team based structure of the organisation.

In conclusion, the following two quotes illustrate the importance of using job descriptions once they are developed:

'Usage will give the job description life, making it a meaningful part of the total management of the organisation' (DeLon, 1994, p. 340).

'Job descriptions that sit on the shelf are worthless. If you take the time to develop them, use them properly as a management tool and make them available to staff.' (Degner, 1995, p.17).

How to Apply for a Library Job?

If you're new to the profession or haven't searched for a library position in a while, this guide is designed for you. It contains some checklists, guidelines, tips and tricks for how to get a library job. Questions candidates should ask are also listed.

Find Job Listings: Here's where you can benefit from the nature of the profession. Librarians have a natural tendency to gather and organize information. As a result there are several ways that you can search for library job advertisements. However, plan ahead when starting your job search! The time between a job's posting and hiring dates can be as much as six months or more.

The best place to start is Combined Library Job Postings. This list contains many combined postings from other sources. It is searchable and even has an RSS feed. Lisjobs.com also offers a professional development e-mail newsletter and a resume posting service (although, in the current employment market, do not expect merely posting a resume anywhere to accomplish much). Library Job Postings on the Internet is another directory of job posting sites. An index of more job listings is available at the Open Directory Project.

E-Mail discussion groups are a good source for job postings. LIBJOBS and LIS-JOBS are two of the more popular ones. Topical groups are also a good place for finding advertisements in a particular field of librarianship.

Another place to check is the major library trade publications, such as Library Journal and American Libraries. There's also related publications, such as The Chronicle of Higher Education for academic library postings or Aviso for archivist jobs.

If you're targeting a specific institution or geographic area, take a look at individual sites. The Folger Shakespeare Library, for example, has their own employment opportunities page. Libweb can help you locate library homepages.

Lastly, if you are a library school student, be sure to check out what career resources your school offers. Many library schools have placement offices which offer help with the application process, including web and e-mail lists for job openings.

Prepare Your Application: Plan ahead in gathering materials that are sometimes required for a library job application. These include writing samples, official copies of academic transcripts and professional references (choose these wisely).

Microsoft Word has a Resume Wizard that can help you create or update your resume. See the book Writing Resumes that Work: A How-to-do-it Manual for Librarians by Robert R. Newlen (ISBN: 1555702635) for guidance on preparing your resume.

Your cover letter explains why your resume is the best match for the position to which you are applying. Take a look at the organization and find out as much information as you can. If you're responding to a paid advertisement, you may need to look elsewhere for a fuller job notice and/or a complete position description. Always prepare a customized (and proofread!) cover letter for each application.

Many institutions are now accepting applications submitted online or via e-mail. Pay attention to each posting's file format preferences (and required application materials!) when dealing with such situations.

Practice Interview Questions: During the phone and in-person interviews you are usually presented with a standard set of questions asked to all candidates. Good reads in preparing for such questions include:

- List of Tested Questions from Indiana University Bloomington Libraries
- 101+ Commonly Asked Interview Questions from an Illinois Library Association conference session
- Having a Successful Job Interview from SLA CapLits

- Frequently Asked Interview Questions University of South Carolina School of Library & Information Science
- Quiddle Blog featuring interview questions

The people you talk to can have varying interviewing styles and some questions may be deliberately designe.

The Phone Interview: If your resume and cover letter make the first round of cuts you are usually contacted for a phone interview. This may be with a single person, or with an entire search committee via a speakerphone (complete with echoes, feedback and not being able to tell who is talking - do your best to remain patient and professional with any possible technical difficulties). When you are given the opportunity to ask questions, take advantage of it. This is your best chance at showing your interest in the position and gathering information for deciding if you want the job. Some of the topics you should be clear on by the end of a phone interview are:

1. Why is this position open?
2. What is your interviewing/hiring time line (and procedure)? When can I expect to hear back from you? It may be quite fruitful to ask, possibly later on in the search process, how many other candidates you are competing with. Some libraries force probationary hires through the formality of applying to keep their job, so knowing if there is an internal candidate may also be very useful. As with all sensitive questions, be tactful but direct in asking for this information.
3. Please describe the organizational structure of the library and where I would fit in it. Who all would I be reporting to and who would report to me? What committees and working groups would I be a member of?
4. Tell me more about the position and its duties. What types of clientele would I be serving and how? If the posting is brief, ask for a full position description.
5. What are you looking for in a candidate? What are some of the challenging and exciting projects that the person in this position will be tackling (both short term and long term)?

Try to get in as many of these questions as you can, but keep in mind that the primary purpose of the phone interview is to select candidates for the next round of interviews.

Before the In-Person Interview: The next step after the phone interview is usually an on site interview. If you have made this next cut and are asked to come in for an interview, there are some extra questions you should have answers to:

1. What is the salary range for this position? [I would consider this a red flag if you have not been told by now, or if you are unfairly asked to provide any salary requirements.]
2. What do I need to bring? A presentation may be required. Ask about available software and hardware. Topics are often vague, so use them to your advantage and deliver a customized talk for discussion on what you know best.
3. It can be interesting to note the differences in how travel arrangements are made. Do they book the flight and pick you up at the airport, or ask you to take a cab? You should never have to pay any of your own expenses, including meals (even if you later turn down an offer). Make sure this is clear before your trip.
4. You shouldn't have to ask for an interview schedule, but make sure you have one ahead of time. You should minimally get to meet everyone you would be working with.

The In-Person Interview: A day-long interview can be an ordeal and health and stamina can be a factor. You may have free cable at the hotel, but still be sure to get a good night's rest! The typical one-day interview - a whirlwind tour from department meeting to department meeting - can be a drain. Make use of break times to recharge (take frequent time-outs in the bathroom if you need to).

Keep in mind all of those "firm handshake"-type interview tips throughout the day. Dress professionally, arrive on time, do your research, don't air dirty laundry, be yourself and be mindful of what you say. Your interview may even begin the night before with an "icebreaker" meal with the screening team, which, while casual, is still part of the interview. Be prepared to meet with large groups and individuals, deal with repeat questions and realize that not everyone may have seen all of your application materials. You could have just finished a presentation on a topic you'd like to discuss, but get asked, "what type of tree would you be?" by an audience member, for example.

R. Lee Hadden has written a post to LIBREF-L on some of the finer points you should notice and ask about during an on site interview. Look for important cues about how polite people are to each other and how much people seem to enjoy their work. The column Top 10 Interview Tips is another useful read. In addition, these are some questions that are likely worth asking:

1. What are the biggest challenges this library is facing? What would you change about the library, if you could?
2. Do you have a healthy collection development/ departmental/overall budget? Are there any cancellation projects or other cutbacks in the works?
3. Ask for an organization chart and formal job description if you don't have one already.
4. Can you describe a typical day's duties? How accurate is the official job description?
5. How bi-directional is the decision making process within your organization? [This one is best asked repeatedly, especially at the end of the day during the obligatory one-on-one with the director.]
6. How productively does this department interact with others? How about the library with the computing centre and other departments? Ask for specific examples. What opportunities would I have to work with others?
7. General policy questions as they relate to your position: do you charge for printing, use censorware, have printed policies for collection development and access to the library, etc..
8. General services questions as they relate to your position: do you offer document delivery, e-mail reference, chat, etc..

9. Use some questions to demonstrate your knowledge of how libraries work: ask the interlibrary loan librarian if they are a net borrower or lender; ask the government documents librarian what percentage of publications they receive; ask the circulation librarian how they handle "lost claims returned" items; ask the automation librarian what systems the web server and OPAC run; ask the collection development librarian about the approval plan; and ask the bindery librarian if they do dissertations or in-house deacidification.
10. What types of official performance reviews and informal feedback would I receive?
11. Is there a union on campus? Many libraries have unionized staff support. Be sure and ask about the nature of any such environment.

Make sure you get a picture of the physical working conditions as well.

1. Where would my desk/office space be located? Show me! Examine the area carefully; you could be spending a lot of time there. Do you have any natural light? Where's the closest bathroom? Is the workspace ergonomic? (*i.e.* is the chair a nice wheeling, reclining one with lumbar support, armrests and height adjustment, or a 70s-era folding chair? I'm not saying you should demand Corinthian Leather... but an office job or repetitive tasks require a comfortable place to sit.)
2. Would you have your own phone extension or remotely-accessible voicemail? Many library positions require a good deal of telephone time. If you've ever worked in an office with shared extensions (and co-workers that take frequent or personal calls) you will realize the importance of this question.
3. If you're on the computer a lot, take a close look at it. How big is the monitor? How durable is the keyboard and mouse? Where's the printer? Is the computer new? What are its specifications? What productivity software is available to you? How fast is the Internet connection?

What level of technical support is available? If this stuff matters to you, you should ask.

4. Is there a break room with amenities (microwave, fridge, tv) that staff socialize in? Where do people eat? What areas of town to people live in and how do they commute? (The Neighborhood Profiles section at Yahoo! has many useful statistics if you are unfamiliar with an area, including a cost of living index against which all salaries should be divided for a fair comparison. Also, if you're looking for places to live, Find Your Spot may give you some ideas.)

Below is another set of questions that you should know the answer to before accepting a job offer. If you have time and to convey your interest, these can also be asked during the interview.

1. Obtain a clear idea of when and how many hours a week you'll be working. It could be forty plus occasional evenings and weekends, or thirty-five including lunch breaks. Get details on lunch and other legally-required breaks, flexibility in working hours and shifts, compensation for overtime if any and when and how you are compensated for working any required nonstandard hours such as evenings and weekends and holidays. You should be comfortable asking about all of this. Make it clear that you are willing to do the work you are paid for, but also convey your understanding of the fundamental philosophy behind the employer-employee relationship: you are paid to work and should not be forced to work for free.
2. Get a written description of all benefits: parking availability and costs, mass transit discounts, available health/dental/vision coverage and premiums and deductibles and co-payments, eligibility to pensions and retirement plan options, flex spending accounts (for tax-free health and dependent care), direct deposit schedules, number of vacation/sick/personal/holiday days awarded and accrued and so on. [These things are best reviewed with a human resources person. The sum of all this can make a big difference when comparing offered salaries.]

3. Do you reimburse association membership and/or travel to conference attendance? [Get specific details in percentages or amounts allowed per year. If you care about professional development, these figures can really add up.]
4. Some places, especially those ascribing to the faculty model of librarianship, have extracurricular requirements for satisfactory job performance and retention. Be sure and get a clear picture on this.

After your interview, many people suggest promptly sending individual thank you notes to the decision-makers. While it might not accomplish anything, it could help you stand out against other candidates. It's also an opportunity for you to reiterate your "hire me" sales pitch, follow-up on any questions you fumbled, or address anything that didn't get covered. If you're comfortable writing a note after your interview, there's little reason not to.

The Job Offer: Ask for time to think over the offer if you need it. Some closing points:

1. The offered salary usually has some wiggle room. It is usually best not to demand anything, just be firm ("an extra few percent would really help... because I have to pay for parking/insurance/mandatory conference attendance..."). Working hours, telecommuting arrangements, additional time off and conference funding models may also be open for negotiation
2. Get a clear answer on when the next salary review (raise) would be.
3. The starting date may be negotiable as well. [It's amazing how the same places that require 60-days notice and take 6 months to conduct a search expect you to break your lease and uproot yourself in 10 days. Demanding expectations like this can be another red flag.]
4. Don't forget moving expenses! Get a clear offer on this before accepting any position.

If you are provided with a written contract, of course you should read it before signing.

Non-traditional Jobs for Special Librarians

The traditional concept of library and librarian is being redefined. As libraries and information media evolve, so too will its workers. The future of information professionals is inversely proportional to their respective ability to adapt to ever-changing media in the professional environment. Non-traditional jobs for special librarians require a fearless, non-superstitious and forward thinking mind-set coupled with an acute ability to self-promote. In order to succeed and flourish in the non-traditional environment, librarians and information professionals must be able to embrace the fluid landscape and nature of information work. This will require the adoption of new perceptions, attitudes, beliefs and the willingness to proactively sell the organizational, research and evaluative expertise that belongs to practitioners of library and information science.

Many companies and private organizations are turning to librarians for expert skills in analyzing, evaluating, organizing and disseminating needed information in the most accessible format. The skills and expertise of librarian and information workers becomes fully realized in the information age. We are moving from an ownership society of information to a shared network of information and information is commodity. Often, the conversion of information to knowledge is the link between success and failure. The critical professional combination of superior finding skills and technological expertise plays an important role in the transfer of knowledge by providing people with access to the information they need and want.

Compensation for such efforts is positive. According to the 1998-1999 Occupational Outlook Handbook: "Slow employment growth, coupled with an increasing number of MLS graduates will result in more applicants competing for fewer jobs. Opportunities will be best for librarians outside the traditional setting."

Begging the question, what are the professional opportunities that lie outside of the traditional setting? The scope and variety is expansive. Some of the possibilities include specialized information centres, government libraries, corporations, law firms, advertising agencies, museums, professional associations, medical centres, hospitals, religious organizations and research laboratories. Technological expertise and capability have opened opportunities in the fields of information systems, publishing, Internet coordination, marketing, database training and web mastering.

Because the type and scope of what can be termed non-traditional is immense, this manual focuses on just a few of the alternatives available for special librarians. The sections are broken down as follows: knowledge management (including consulting and information brokerage), telecommuting, bibliotherapy and information work with the physically and mentally challenged. The professional opportunities for information workers are endless and the prospects will continue to grow as technology transforms the non-traditional into the traditional. A bibliography is included at the end of the handbook for further reading and research.

Knowledge Management, Information Brokerage and Consulting : The ultimate value of documentation within an organization lies in the ability to capture, retain and transfer knowledge to those who need it. In the corporate world, the most critical asset of any organization is knowledge. The management of that asset should be one of the most critical concerns of any business. Each and every decision made within an organization is dependent on knowledge. The need for quality solutions to information overload, time constraints of users and sheer complexity are some of the reasons users turn to an outside agent for information. Better and more reliable information will distinguish itself from lesser products and people will pay to save themselves time and frustration. The relationship between effective knowledge management and the success or failure of a business lends itself to the creation of a new breed of librarians and information specialists. The possibilities for a special librarian who effectively markets his/ her organizational, research and knowledge management skills will have a place in the information driven future. Because of these skills, many librarians are assuming entirely new positions within their respective organizations becoming consultants, information brokers and knowledge managers.

Effective consultants, information brokers and knowledge managers collect and evaluate the most applicable and accurate data for the client. They stay actively informed and abreast of all information happenings within and related to the client's professional environment. Consultants and information brokers may be involved with creating databases, web pages and Intranets composed of the indexed and abstracted news relevant to the client. To succeed, these professionals should save clients time, provide high quality information, supply new solutions to organizational information needs and offer new packaging. It is no longer enough to present the user with a pile of documents as an answer to a question. Information professionals must present the best possible information in a timely manner in the best possible format for the client. Besides offering a superior product, knowledge workers must rely on marketing skills, ingenuity and networking to keep their services in demand. The body of research and practice in library and information science used for classification and knowledge organization will be vital to an information-inundated business.

Joanne Wleklinski, Knowledge Management Specialist (and former librarian) offers some professional tips for success in non-traditional information roles. Some of these include: "don't focus on one department--get out and learn about everything, see the company from all different angles, deliver research by hand, develop personal working relationships, synthesize research and writing roles, synthesize information into knowledge and above all else, be flexible, multi-dimensional and proactive."

The skills of the librarian naturally lend themselves to a myriad of professional settings that require efficient and productive use of information. In light of this inclination, willing adaptability seems to be the deciding factor for successful integration into non-traditional environments. "Evolve into useful agents, evangelize your capabilities, work alongside the people, never let a false sense of traditionalism push you into a rigid, self-imposed isolation. It can leave you as a librarian chasing the information revolution instead of leading it, as librarians should." (Wleklinski 10.)

Telecommuting: Telecommuting is another professional option open for special librarians. Advanced technology for telecommuting allows librarian and information workers to work from home or any mobile location by remote. This is the alternative workplace, the combination of non-traditional work practices, settings and locations that is beginning to supplement traditional offices. Some 30 to 40 million people in the US are now either telecommuters or home-based workers. Emerging jobs for librarians involving knowledge management and traditional jobs such and indexing, abstracting and cataloging can currently be achieved through telecommuting. That is, all workflow (including input, output and the majority of communications) are handled by computer technologies away from a centralized office.

Moving the work to the worker has many benefits for both employer and employee. Some benefits of telecommuting for the employer include: reducing current and future costs associated with real estate (property, leases and overhead), increased productivity, increased recruitment and retention rates, increased customer satisfaction and consolidation/reallocation of space. Employees in the alternative workplace tend to devote less time and energy to typical office routines and more to tasks, clients and patrons.

The benefits to the employee include fewer distractions, less downtime, no commute, flexibility, more personal time and having the freedom to set up workspace according to personal preference. Telecommuting employees are covered under the Worker's Compensation Act if injured while performing work responsibilities. Generally, equipment is provided and maintained by the employer, although some allow employees to utilize their own equipment. Telecommuters are provided the same help from systems staff as the traditional office for any trouble-shooting questions or consultations. Often, portions of company savings produced by telecommuting are earmarked for dividends to enhance employee commitment and loyalty.

Telecommuting programmes that are successful do not leave their telecommuters without support. One needs more than a laptop and a cellular phone to be effective in a telecommuting environment. Teamwork/group cohesion is still a very important part of the work environment. Telecommuting can build teamwork and organizational cohesion through communicational technology by enabling immediate communication with co-workers and shared access to information. Shared access empowers all employees. The collective nature of the telecommuting environment lends an egalitarian quality to the workplace.

The ability to excel in the telecommuting environment depends on an array of new communication skills and competencies. Telecommuting programmes must be committed to success by offering relevant training, appropriate equipment and flexible administrative support. Flexibility/adaptability, respect for personal time/priorities and a commitment to using technology for improving performance characterize the workplace of the future. In the information age, the alternative workplace offers a profound opportunity to benefit the individual, organization and enterprise.

Bibliotherapy: Bibliotherapy is a treatment technique used by information professionals to make therapeutic use of selected reading materials for clients and patrons. Through the guided reading of written materials, patrons/clients are helped to gain an understanding or insight into solving problems relevant to therapeutic needs thereby affecting attitude and behavioural changes. Health and wellness professionals rely on the librarians' knowledge of literature to recommend books and other informational material to help reach goals set forth in the therapy process. Bibliotherapy is usually performed collaboratively with health, psychology and information professionals. Bibliotherapy is used in public, private and independent health resource information centres, libraries and in conjunction with traditional forms of psychotherapy. Librarians working as bibliotherapists strive to reflect all aspects of applicable literature (fiction and non-fiction), current treatment, diagnosis and recovery for a wide variety of mental and physical health needs.

Bibliotherapy should not be viewed as a single approach to treatment but rather as an adjunct to other therapies. As with most therapies, bibliotherapy is not a cure-all that will automatically influence attitudes or behaviours in the desired direction. But, bibliotherapy as a practice, has the ability to reach people who may not otherwise seek traditional help. For those reluctant to disclose their situations and for families and friends who wish to understand and offer help to those suffering, the library can offer a wealth of information and support in a private environment. Bibliotherapy is used to address a wide variety of topics including: learning disabilities, sexual abuse, drug and alcohol abuse, mental illness, disease etc.

Bibliotherapy is especially appropriate in the modern world because it provides a safe way to confront dilemmas. Through the selected use of literature, clients have an opportunity to identify, relive, compensate and solve problems in a controlled manner. Bibliotherapy contributes a crucial connection to those in need by showing they are not alone in facing their particular problem. The controlled and selected use of professionally chosen literature for clients helps develop self-concept through identification and increased knowledge of any given problem, which lends itself to the development of more appropriate and healthier coping skills.

Throughout time, books have been used as powerful tools with which to guide thinking, strengthen character, shape behaviour, inform and now, to solve problems. Bibliotherapy is a very unobtrusive method of helping those in need. It offers a safe and vicarious way for people to work through their difficulties and the faculty to reach a wider audience than traditional therapies. The wealth of excellent resources currently available, coupled with heightened cultural interest in mental and physical health, has led to an increase in the popularity and practice of bibliotherapy. Professionals involved with bibliotherapy find it to be a rewarding career, as the benefits of bibliotherapy are many and the drawbacks very few.

Working with the Mentally and Physically Challenged: In July 1990, Congress enacted Public Law 101-336--the Americans with Disabilities Act (ADA). The ADA is a federal effort to prohibit discrimination based on one's disability. ADA laws apply to many private and public employers and facilities.

The ADA has done much to heighten public awareness to the needs of those with disabilities by requiring facilities to provide equal access. According to the ADA "public accommodations must provide auxiliary aids and services to individuals with vision or hearing impairments or other individuals with disabilities so that they can have an equal opportunity to participate or benefit, unless an undue burden would result." While this is a huge step forward, the undefined "undue burden" shifts most concerns and changes toward the issue of building access compliance alone.

This is of particular interest to the library and librarian who recognize that further measures must be utilized to reach this portion of the population. It is great to be able to get in to the library building, but what if once you get in, the information you are looking for is inadequate or simply not there? Sadly, that is the case in most public libraries. There are so many people with disabilities who never find applicable resources because of a lack of connected information.

This can be attributed, in part, to the fact that the ADA does "not specifically require a public accommodation [such as a library or museum] to alter its inventory to include accessible or special goods that are designed for, or facilitate use by individuals with disabilities" However, "a public accommodation shall order accessible or special goods at the request of the individual with a disability, if, in the normal course of its operation, it makes special orders on request for unstocked goods and if the accessible or special goods can be obtained from a supplier with whom the public accommodation customarily does business." (Federal Register 1991,36.707)

Herein lies the problem. How can you order materials that you do not know exist? Moreover, many of the applicable collection items for the mentally and physically challenged are not found in the catalogues of traditional library suppliers. Over 50 million Americans live with a disability that interferes with everyday activities, approximately 20% of the population in any given community in the US has some form of disability and people with disabilities constitute the largest minority in the country. One can quickly see the importance of specialized library and information centres devoted to this population. Most facilities specializing in library services to the disabled operate in conjunction with local agencies, private organizations, or as a separate library within a larger library facility.

These institutions provide a critical link between the client and needed information. Special libraries, in a dedicated environment, can house and supplement helpful resources that this segment may not be exposed to otherwise. Special librarians can play an instrumental role in breaking the information barrier by providing good, positive, practical information to help the physically and mentally challenged live autonomously. Librarians working in an environment devoted to the mentally and physically challenged should work closely with local organizations to promote and market collective resources. Such cooperation can result in many supplemental programmemes and workshops designed to inform the disabled community about issues such as legal rights, educational programmemes, scholarships, job opportunities, assistive technology and involvement with local advocacy groups.

Special libraries and information centres for the physically and mentally challenged grant exposure to material that is understandable, accessible and appropriate for this population. The ideal of providing equal access should encompass the effort to bring people who might otherwise be isolated into the body of the community.

The need for librarians to mend this information breach is acute. Librarians who work and thrive in this environment strive to avoid stereotypes, assumptions, ignorance and poor disability etiquette. Programmes and services should provide clients with the capabilities to proceed with their endeavours as independently as possible. With appropriate information, accessibility and outreach, special libraries and information centres can help these individuals bridge the information gap to promote better living.

3

Job Descriptions

Sample Library Job Descriptions

Assistant Librarian Sample 1

Position: Assistant Librarian

Accountable To: Head Librarian

Summary of Work: Under the general supervision of the Head Librarian, performs professional and technical work in operating and maintaining the public library.

Job Characteristics:

Nature of Work: varied and complex duties in processing materials and public requests related to library operation.

Personal Contacts: frequent contact with public; daily coordination of activities with supervisor.

Supervision Received: Minimal.

Supervision Exercised: Direction of the activities of substitutes and volunteers in conjunction with the Head Librarian:

Areas of job accountability and performance:

Checks out and reshelves books and maintains stacks

Receives application for and grants library cards

Renews and cancels library cards on a yearly basis

Answers questions concerning reference materials, periodicals and books

Assists patrons in operation of microfilm reader and photocopier

Issues overdue notices and collects fines

Maintains daily activities worksheet

Instructs students and others in library use

Assists in research requests

Organizes local history collection

Helps organize special exhibits

Delivers books to shut-ins

Maintains a tranquil library environment

Conducts yearly inventory

Attends workshops and maintains membership in professional organizations

Performs other related duties as required.

Job Requirements

Knowledge: This position requires a working knowledge of library principles, organization, operations and procedures and reference materials and books.

Skills and Abilities: This position requires skills in inventory, record-keeping and operation of library equipment; ability to perform a variety of duties without supervision, to communicate orally and in writing, to follow written and verbal instructions; ability to establish and maintain effective working relationships with employees, supervisors and the public.

Education and Experience: The above knowledge, skills and abilities are typically acquired through a combination of education and experience equivalent to a bachelor's degree in liberal arts or library science and some experience in library operations.

Job Performance Standards: Evaluation of this position will be based primarily upon the preceding job description requirements and duties. Examples of job performance criteria include the following:

Performs assigned duties

Assists in providing library services

Maintains accurate records of ILL requests and postage

Prepares and submits accurate reports

Performs supervisory function in absence of Head Librarian

Maintains contemporary knowledge of library practices

Observes work hours

Demonstrates punctuality

Displays tact and patience when dealing with the public

Establishes and maintains effective working relationships with fellow employees, supervisors and the public

Dresses professionally

Maintains the display case monthly (contacts other clubs etc.)

Performs ILL for Patrons

Assistant Librarian Sample 2 - For Community College

Position: Assistant Librarian

Department: Library

Accountable To: Library Director

Summary of Work: Position develops, maintains and provides access to and instruction in library resources and information at Dawson Community College. Provides information services to faculty, administration, students, staff and community.

Job Characteristics

Nature of Work: This position performs administrative and technical duties requiring accuracy and attention to detail in the operation of the college library. Position is required to work a split shift which results in evening and sometimes weekend work. Must be flexible to cover additional hours usually working over 40 hours per week. Fills in when the Library Director is absent. Must be able to lift and shelve books and have access to upper and lower library shelves. Maintains confidentiality of sensitive information.

Personal Contacts: Continuous contact with library patrons including students, staff, administrators, faculty and the community.

Supervision Received: Position is mainly self-directed with special or immediate assignments from the supervisor.

Supervision Exercised: Supervision of from 6-12 work study students per year; each averages nine hours per week. Trains students in the various library functions. Disciplines and terminates, if necessary.

Essential Functions: Position requires ability to: communicate orally and in writing; supervise and train work study students; read written material; order and process books and materials; apply computer knowledge including current word processing software and Internet searching; maintain catalogue; maintain circulation database; complete inter-library loan requests; keep library organized and tidy; calculate; maintain records; type and file; assist users; and operate office machines.

Areas of Job Accountability and Performance:

- Implement and provide assistance in accessing learning resources to patrons.
- Provide technical services including database management of automated catalogue, circulation system and OCLC/WLN service; Interlibrary Loan services and periodical management.

Cataloging:

- Generate, classify and process orders for new acquisitions.
- Physically process all new acquisitions.
- Maintain cost account of all acquisitions.
- Transfer and edit electronic records to and from OCLC/WLN, Library of Congress (LC) and the local database while maintaining integrity and accuracy of authority records.

Circulation:

- Maintain and update circulation database and resolve related problems.
- Train student assistants to follow established circulation policies and procedures.
- Set up report modules to print overdue notices and other reports and statistics.

OCLC/WLN (Online Computer Library Centre):

- Submit accurate and consistent holding records for all new acquisitions to the OCLC/WLN network and attach our call number; send quarterly.
- Make corrections and/or update our holdings records.

Interlibrary Loan:

- Directs all inter-library loans from patron request through loan completion and maintains records.
- Produces required reports for statistics and state reimbursement.
- Uses bibliographic and other electronic databases to effect the interlibrary loans.
- Chooses appropriate, cost-effective and timely sources for meeting ILL needs; uses and supervises the use of computer equipment, copies and fax.

Periodicals:

- Receipts and processes journals, newspapers and other periodicals.
- Maintains physical periodical collection; replaces damaged and missing materials.
- Assists users in the use of periodicals.
- Assists with Internet accessible journals and indexing.
- Maintains periodical records in the shared database and WLN.

Other duties:

- Assists in development, review and evaluation of library resources, policies and procedures.
- Maintains statistics of library operations for internal and external reporting.
- Attend training as technology changes.
- Assists with answering the telephone in the evenings for the college.
- Manages the faculty reserve shelves.
- Oversees and assists with equipment use, videos and rentals.

- Does book repair.
- Orders and processes materials and supplies for the Library.
- Handles materials and some tests for the Distance Learning Centre.
- Assigns work study duties, trains and supervises.
- Performs other related duties as required.

Job Requirements

Knowledge: This position requires a knowledge of: modern practices and procedures for researching, accessing and maintaining library materials and resources; computerized library systems; use of office machines and A/V equipment; and current word processing programmes.

Skills: This position requires skills in use of: computers, office machines, A/V equipment and skills in maintaining databases and critical thinking skills.

Abilities: This position requires the ability to: organize and prioritize duties; be self-directed; supervise and train students; work evening hours; be on call when work study students work evening hours; solve people and computer problems; do research; communicate effectively orally and in writing; follow verbal and written instructions; work with numerous interruptions; learn complex database systems; handle stress; sit for long periods of time at computer; establish effective working relationships with fellow employees, students, supervisors and the public.

Education and Experience: The above knowledge, skills and abilities are typically acquired through a combination of education and experience equivalent to:

- A minimum of an Associate degree in library science preferred.
- Two or more years of experience working in a library.
- Experience with computers and office machines.
- Must be certified by the state in interlibrary loan procedures.

Job Performance Standards: Evaluation of this position will be based primarily upon performance of the preceding requirements and duties. Examples of job performance criteria include, but are not limited to, the following:

- Performs assigned duties.
- Demonstrates knowledge of modern library practices and procedures.
- Keeps abreast of new technology related to library functions.
- Capably provides library services to patrons.
- Capably trains and supervises work-study students.
- Competently maintains computerized records and databases.
- Capably assists patrons to find information and materials.
- Capably assists with phones and other duties for the college.
- Provides for an organized, tidy library.
- Maintains accurate and timely records.
- Prepares and submits accurate and timely reports.
- Deals tactfully and courteously with the public.
- Observes work hours.
- Demonstrates punctuality.
- Maintains strict confidentiality regarding library usage and faxes.
- Establishes and maintains effective working relationships with fellow employees, supervisors and the public.

Children's Librarian Sample 2

Assistant Librarian Sample 3

Position: Assistant Librarian/Children's Librarian

Department: Library

Accountable to: Library Director; Library Board

Summary of Work: Under general guidance assesses, selects, processes and catalogues library materials suitable for children and young adults; responsible for Storytime for preschoolers; administers annual Summer Reading Programme; prepares programmes for grade school classes each school year; maintains children's card catalogue (currently paper-based, soon to be electronic); assists library patrons with reference questions; assists library patrons with routine computer and Internet use questions; staffs circulation desk, performing routine library clerical tasks associated therewith; other duties as assigned.

Job Characteristics

Nature of Work: This position functions as assistant librarian and children's librarian as well as performing technical library tasks. Position organizes and maintains library materials according to established procedures, assists patrons, performs other duties related to library operations.

Personal Contacts: Daily contact with public, school children, other library staff, other town employees, library board members.

Supervision Received: Minimal supervision; guidance as needed.

Supervision Exercised: May supervise seasonal clerk, volunteers.

Essential Functions: Position requires knowledge of children's and young adult library materials; ability to communicate effectively orally and in writing; ability to work with the general public; ability to type, work with library databases, computer software and wordprocessing; ability to navigate the Internet; ability to retrieve and return books to shelves; ability to maintain files and records in an orderly manner.

Areas of Job Accountability and Performance: Maintains and improves children's library; communicates with school teachers and students; performs Storytime; composes and prepares routine correspondence; assists with annual budget preparation; maintains library annual statistics; assists library patrons; issues overdue notices; orders and processes interlibrary loan materials, maintaining such records as necessary; supervises volunteers and library clerk as needed.

Job Requirements

Knowledge: Position requires basic knowledge of library methods, practices and procedures and children's books and literature.

Skills: Position requires skills in computer use, basic typing, word processing; filing, basic bookkeeping; and operation of library and office equipment.

Abilities: Position requires the ability to: work with children and children's library materials; shelve books; maintain a filing and catalogue system according to standard library procedures; to deal tactfully with patrons; to be dependable, efficient and honest; to communicate effectively orally and in writing; to follow verbal and written instructions; and to establish effective working relationships with fellow employees, supervisors and the public.

Education and Experience: The above knowledge, skills and abilities are typically acquired through a combination of experience and education equivalent to a college degree. Experience working with the public is required. Experience in elementary education, or a school or public library is highly recommended.

Job Performance Standards: Evaluation of the position will be based primarily on performance of the preceding requirements and duties. Examples of job performance criteria include but are not limited to the following:

- Performs assigned duties;
- Demonstrates a knowledge and understanding of children's library operations and procedures;
- Handles library materials with care and diligence;
- Adheres to state law influencing the duties and responsibilities of the position;
- Provides useful and cooperative assistance to patrons;
- Works well independently,
- Maintains accurate and timely records;
- Prepares and submits accurate and timely reports;
- Displays consideration and cooperation when dealing with the public;

- Observes work hours;
- Demonstrates punctuality;
- Establishes and maintains effective working relationships with fellow employees; supervisors and the public.

Branch Librarian

Branch Librarian-I

Nature of Work: The position in this class functions as the paraprofessional librarian in charge of a small branch library in the County library system.

The tasks performed entail responsibility for the complete operation of the respective library. Duties include the circulation of library materials, the registration of library patrons, the furnishing of information to library users and oversight of library building maintenance, repairs and cleaning.

Work is performed under the general supervision of the library director or an assigned library supervisor and is reviewed on the basis of conferences, reports and patron satisfaction.

An employee in this classification has contact with local Government personnel, community groups and Friends of the Library in tailoring library services to the needs of the community patrons served. Close contact is maintained with the headquarters library, particularly with regard to reference questions and the coordination of circulated materials between the main library and the respective branch. Direction and guidance is exercised over part-time staff, volunteers and programme workers. Work is performed in the Bigfork branch of the library system.

Distinguishing Characteristics: This is the first level of a two-level series. The position in this class is distinguished from positions in the Branch Librarian II by the size of the branch library, which is the smallest, in terms of patrons and circulation of the three branch libraries of the Flathead County Library System.

Representative Examples of Work: Only major tasks are identified for most positions; refer to position description for detailed listing of duties.

Develops and selects library materials for the branch; provides patron services in locating library materials and checking library materials in and out.

Responds to patrons' reference questions by advising where materials are located; places reserved materials on request; teaches patrons how to place library materials on hold.

Answers telephone requests; demonstrates operation of DYNIX library computer information system.

Meets with building officials to coordinate building and security matters.

Organizes and conducts children's story time; assists in selecting books and other materials; conducts library tours.

Processes applications for library cards; notifies patrons of overdue books; collects fines.

Oversees and participates in the shelving of books, records, magazines and other items; creates or oversees the placement of book displays and seasonal decorations.

Trains volunteers in library work.

Prepares monthly statistics on patrons served and fine monies.

Arranges for cleaning of the branch; advises proper officials when maintenance or repair of facilities is required.

Performs related work as assigned.

Selection Factors: These factors will be the basis for selecting the most qualified applicants to be interviewed. Applicants selected for employment must satisfactorily demonstrate possession of these factors during and after a prescribed probationary period for continued employment.

Knowledge of:

- o modern library principles, methods and procedures.
- o basic library reference materials and procedures.
- o local reader interests, books and authors.

Skill In: operating a computer keyboard, various library equipment and the FAX machine.

Ability to:

- o work independently.
- o carry out work tasks independently with a minimum of supervision.
- o establish and maintain effective working relationships with library patrons, local government officials, local community groups, local Friends of the Library groups and employees.
- o lift and carry up to fifty pounds.
- o learn and abide by County Library policies and procedures.

General Recruitment Indicators: Person applying for a position in this class should have the following experience and/ or training.

Two years experience as a library technical or branch assistant; or any equivalent combination of experience and training which indicates possession of the knowledge, skills and abilities listed.

Branch Librarian-II

Nature of Work: The position in this class functions as the paraprofessional librarian in charge of the largest branch libraries in the County library system.

The tasks performed entail responsibility for the day-to-day operation of the respective branch library. Duties include the circulation of library materials, the registration of library patrons, the furnishing of information to library users and oversight of library building maintenance, repairs and cleaning.

Work is performed under the general supervision of the library director or an assigned library supervisor and is reviewed on the basis of conferences, reports and patron satisfaction. Supervision is exercised over a small staff of branch library assistants and various volunteers.

Employees in this classification have extensive contact with the respective city administration, community groups and Friends of the Library in tailoring library services to the needs of the community patrons served. Close contact is maintained with the headquarters library, particularly with regard to reference questions and the coordination of circulated materials between the headquarters library and the respective branches.

Responsibility is for the operation and direction of either of two branches of the of the County Library System.

Distinguishing Characteristics: This is the second level of a two-level series. Positions are distinguished from the lower level Branch Librarian I by the size of the library facility and staff, higher patron and usage, greater circulation of materials and greater decision making responsibilities.

Representative Examples of Work: Only major tasks are identified for most positions; refer to position description for detailed listing of duties.

Supervises and evaluates staff; priorities staff assignments; participates in providing patron service in locating library materials and checking library materials in and out.

Develops and selects library materials for the branch; provides patron services in locating library materials and checking library materials in and out.

Responds to patrons' reference questions by advising where materials are located or in requesting material from the main library; prepares patrons' other library requests from main library; transmits patrons' special requests to main library.

Answers telephone requests: demonstrates operation of photocopier, of DYNIX library computer information system and other library equipment.

Organizes and supervises children's story time; assists in selecting books and other materials; conducts library tours.

Processes applications for library cards; notifies patrons of overdue books; collects fines.

Shelves books, records, magazines and other items; organizes and files book cards; creates book displays and seasonal decorations.

Trains staff and volunteers in library work.

Prepares daily and monthly statistics on circulation, patrons served, fine money and donations.

Performs minor cleaning such as dusting; advises proper officials when cleaning, maintenance or repair of facilities is required.

Performs related work, as assigned.

Selection Factors: These factors will be the basis for selecting the most qualified applicants to be interviewed. Applicants selected for employment must satisfactorily demonstrate possession of these factors during and after a prescribed probationary period for continued employment.

Knowledge of:

o modern library principles, methods and procedures.

o basic library reference materials and procedures.

o local reader interests, books and authors.

Skill In: operating a computer keyboard, various library equipment and the FAX machine.

Ability to:

- work with considerable independence and make sound decisions in the operation of the branch.
- survey the work of a small group of paraprofessional employees and volunteers.
- establish and maintain effective working relationships with library patrons, local government officials, local community groups, local Friends of the Library groups and employees.
- lift and carry up to fifty pounds.
- learn and abide by Flathead County Library policies and procedures.
- become and remain a certified librarian by the State of Montana.

General Recruitment Indicators: Person applying for a position in this class should have the following experience and/or training.

Four years experience as a library technical or branch assistant; or successful completion of library science course work may be substituted for up to two years of the experience;

or any equivalent combination of experience and training which indicates possession of the knowledge, skills and abilities listed.

Children's Librarian

Sample 1

Position Description

Position: Children's Librarian

Department: County Library

Accountable To: Library Director

Summary of Work: Provides general library services for the young library users; provides special library services such as summer reading programmes, weekly story time including crafts and other programmes that enhance the lives and promotes reading to young library users,

Job Characteristics

Nature of Work: This position performs professional duties requiring adherence to standards of accuracy, timeliness, tact and confidentiality. Position requires ability to move and shelve heavy books. Position works mainly with children and requires working varied work schedule including evenings and weekends. Consequence of errors may result in dissatisfied library users and loss of time to find and correct mistakes.

Personal Contacts: Continual contact with the children and the general public. Coordinates duties with other employees and supervisor to complete tasks.

Supervision Received: Direction from Library Director.

Essential Functions: Position requires ability to communicate orally and in writing, retrieve and return books to shelves, type, calculate, read written material, maintain files, mend books, operate a computer, operate library machines and equipment. Skills to work well with a group of children or with one child. Maintains and applies a knowledge of library automation systems.

Areas of Job Accountability and Performance: Strives to meet the objectives of the library as established by the Board.

Organizes and gives tours of the library and its services to all students and groups of young library users. Enhances the programmes of the local schools by providing consultative and classroom services. Supervises the daily operation of the children's section of the library; organizes attractive book displays and sets the children's section of the library in order to attract young library users and encourage reading.

Acts as lead worker in promoting and planning programmes for the young library users. Maintains the on-going programme of special events for children such as story time and summer reading. Provides direction to library staff and volunteers as they shelve and assist in the children's section. Maintains circulation records and reports as required by the library director and/or other agencies.

Assists with collection management of the children's section, including inventory, assessing, weeding, purchasing, adding gifts and technical processing. Train young library users to search for information by following an appropriate inquiry process using books and/or electronics resources.

Serves all library users by assisting with reference questions as needed; answers the phone as needed. Works at the circulation desk when assigned. Checks in library materials and shelves materials. Performs related duties as required.

Job Requirements

Knowledge: This position requires a thorough knowledge of library practices, procedures and techniques; knowledge of children's literature and children's reading programmes and activities; a working knowledge of the laws, regulations and departmental policies pertaining to library services.

Skills: This position requires skills in dealing with children, providing activities and in the use of computers and library equipment.

Abilities: Position requires ability to: be creative, have imagination; read aloud; direct craft activities; supervise assistants and volunteers; establish good rapport with children; establish discipline; pay attention to accuracy; work with interruptions; maintain effective working relationships with fellow employees, other agencies and the public; communicate clearly and effectively verbally and in writing.

Education and Experience: The above knowledge, skills, ability are usually acquired through a combination of education and/or experience equivalent to:

- A Bachelor's Degree with library and/or literature credits.
- Experience working in a public library is preferred.
- Current state certification is preferred.
- Strong interest in reading preferred.

Job Performance Standards: Evaluation of this position will be based primarily upon performance of the preceding requirements and duties. Examples of job performance criteria include, but are not limited to, the following:

- Performs assigned duties.
- Meets the objectives of the library as established by the Board.
- Competently provides programmes and activities for young library users.
- Provides for attractive displays and settings to encourage reading.
- Efficiently processes books as needed.
- Competently recommends purchases for children's collection.
- Effectively assists all library patrons in the use of the library.
- Maintains confidentiality of sensitive information.
- Maintains accurate and timely records.
- Deals tactfully and courteously with the public.
- Keeps work areas neat.
- Observes work hours.
- Demonstrates punctuality.
- Establishes and maintains effective working relationships with fellow employees, supervisors and the public.

Sample 3

Final Draft Approved By Library Trustees

Class Title: Library System Operator II - Children's Services

Accountable To: Library Director

Primary Objective of Position: Under the general direction of the Library Director, works collaboratively with other Library staff members to deliver professional quality library service to the public. Has primary responsibility for general and specialized service to children and bookmobile patrons. Has special responsibility for all children's programmeming. Shares with the Library Director responsibility for the selection of children's and bookmobile books and other relevant information resources in all formats including the internet. As a member of the Library staff is required to keep abreast of all Library activities and priorities, with particular focus on how these priorities might affect responsibilities and activities within own position. Performs all routine library functions including book and periodical shelving.

Major Areas of Accountability and Performance

Works collaboratively with other Library staff members to plan, organize and coordinate a comprehensive children's library programme and bookmobile trips in a rotating schedule.

In collaboration with the rest of the Library staff provides general and specialized reference and readers advisory service, library orientation, programmeming and instruction specifically for children. Devises search strategies to accommodate children and bookmobile patrons using information resources including the internet, WLN and the book and periodical collections of the Library.

Is responsible for the safe operation of the bookmobile and the personal safety of each bookmobile patron on each trip.

Is responsible for routine record keeping and maintenance of the bookmobile.

Collects and provides statistical reports in areas of responsibility.

In the absence of the Library Director, can assume operational responsibility for the Library's daily operations.

Monitors, selects from the Library's collections and dispenses library materials used on weekly bookmobile trips and during children's programmes. Handles in a timely fashion all patron requests for materials.

Performs routine updating functions of the Library's Dynix circulation records. Oversees creation of overdue notices and bills from the Dynix automated circulation system.

Supports overall Library operations and services through projects and other duties as appropriate and assigned. Actively supports Library colleagues, Library service goals and the Library's mission.

As possible, participates in state wide, regional and national activities of the library profession.

Supervision - Responsibility for the Work of Others: Supervises as assigned staff, volunteers, work study students, community service workers and summer youth workers, including assigning work, training, monitoring and evaluating assigned work.

Education, Training and Experience Requirements: Bachelor's Degree or two years (minimum) of experience in an automated library preferred, including familiarity with use of computerized library resources; affinity for cooperation and collaboration; good interpersonal, verbal and written skills important; service orientation essential; comfort with a varied pace, overlapping tasks, details and change. Class B1 drivers license required.

Examples of Performance Criteria and Qualifications: Effectively meets the public and assists in the effective use of library and bookmobile resources.

Maintains collaborative working relationships with fellow employees.

Maintains a cordial and professional relationship with the public.

Within the parameters of position responsibilities, proposes new or changed policies and procedures to accomplish own responsibilities, related operations and the Library's mission.

Supports overall Library operations and services through projects, training and other duties as appropriate and assigned.

Opens the Library building and prepares it for each day's use.

Operates the bookmobile in a safe, well maintained and prudent manner.

At library closing times, correctly shuts down all equipment including computers, secures the building and assures lock-up.

Circulation Librarian

Sample 1

Position Description

Position: Circulation Librarian

Department: County Library

Accountable To: Library Director

Summary of Work: Maintains and delivers library services for the community; serves as lead worker for responsibilities of the circulation desk; facilitates the circulation of library materials and maintains circulation statistics and borrowers records. Compiles statistics and annual reports according to the needs of the library director and staff. Assists the director in maintaining computers and automation system to perform at optimum level.

Job Characteristics

Nature of Work: This position performs professional duties requiring adherence to standards of accuracy, timeliness, tact and confidentiality. Position requires ability to move and shelve heavy books. Position works varying work schedule including evenings and weekends. Consequence of error's may result in dissatisfied library users and loss of time to find and correct mistakes.

Personal Contacts: Continual and demanding contact with the public. Coordinates duties with other employees and supervisor to complete tasks.

Supervision Received: Direction from Library Director.

Essential Functions: Position requires ability to communicate orally and in writing, retrieve and return books to shelves, type, file, supervise, calculate, read written material, maintain records, mend books, operate a computer, prepare reports, write correspondence, operate library machines and equipment. Demonstrates a thorough knowledge of library automation systems.

Areas of Job Accountability and Performance: Strives to meet the objectives of the library as established by the Board.

Provides direction to other library employees, student workers and volunteers in the circulation department. Orders general library supplies as needed.

Serves all library users by assisting with reference questions, works the circulation desk according to the assigned schedule, follows routine procedures. Answers the telephone as needed. Performs other related duties as required.

Performs or delegates the following daily activities: check library material in and out; shelve books; contact library users with overdue materials and materials on hold.

Organizes circulation and overdue notice procedures. Assures all library users are properly registered to check out library material. Prepares monthly circulation reports as required by the library director and/or other agencies. Generates cataloging, system, or circulation reports according to the needs of the library director and staff.

Assists with the maintenance, implementation and development of the library's automation system and network. Troubleshoots system and search stations. Follows maintenance schedule to clear files, to clean and keep all work stations free from dust, to monitor the tap process and to back-up the system. Trains library users to search the World Wide Web (Internet).

Assists with collection management, including inventory, assessing, weeding, purchasing, evaluating gifts and technical processing. Evaluate books for bindery or mend in house. Supervise and train staff and volunteers to assist with mending books.

Job Requirements

Knowledge: This position requires a thorough knowledge of library practices, procedures and techniques, a working knowledge of the laws, regulations and departmental policies pertaining to library services, knowledge of business English, grammar, operation of office machines, computers, search stations, word processors and automation system.

Skills: This position requires skills in dealing with the public; skills in writing; skills in the use of computers and library equipment.

Abilities: Position requires ability to: work well with the public; complete tasks; pay attention to accuracy; work with interruptions; maintain confidentiality; stay abreast on new procedures affecting library and services; supervise assistants and volunteers; prepare reports; maintain effective working relationships with fellow employees, other agencies and the public; communicate clearly and effectively verbally and in writing.

Education and Experience: The above knowledge, skills, ability are usually acquired through a combination of education and/or experience equivalent to:

- A Bachelor's Degree and three years of experience working in a public library is preferred.
- Current state certification is preferred.
- Strong interest in reading preferred.

Job Performance Standards: Evaluation of this position will be based primarily upon performance of the preceding requirements and duties. Examples of job performance criteria include, but are not limited to, the following:

- Performs assigned duties.
- Meets the objectives of the library as established by the Board.
- Competently oversees responsibilities of the circulation desk.
- Competently maintains circulation statistics and borrowers' records.

- Effectively assists all library patrons in the use of the library.
- Maintains confidentiality of sensitive information.
- Prepares accurate and timely reports.
- Deals tactfully and courteously with the public.
- Keeps work areas neat.
- Observes work hours.
- Demonstrates punctuality.
- Establishes and maintains effective working relationships with fellow employees, supervisors and the public.
- Operates and deploys all modules and functions of the automation system, computers and search stations.

Library Clerk

Sample 1

Position Description

Position: Library Clerk

Department: County Library

Accountable To: Library Director

Summary of Work: Performs various duties as assigned in the operation of the library including assisting with circulation duties, processing library materials and assisting where needed. Makes decisions on how best to assist the library users.

Job Characteristics

Nature of Work: This position performs semi-skilled duties requiring adherence to standards of accuracy, timeliness, tact and confidentiality. Position requires ability to move and shelve heavy books. Position works varying work schedule and includes some evenings and weekends. Consequence of errors may result in dissatisfied library users and loss of time to find and correct mistakes.

Personal Contacts: Continual and demanding contact with the public. Coordinates duties with other employees and supervisor to complete tasks.

Supervisions Received: Direction from Library Director and other regular staff members.

Essential Functions: Position requires ability to communicate orally and in writing, retrieve and return books to shelves, type, read written material and operate a computer, Maintains operating knowledge of the library automation system.

Areas of Job Accountability and Performance:

Strives to meet the objectives of the library as established by the Board.

Serves all library users at the circulation desk and answers any reference questions or refers the library users to someone who is able to assist them.

Maintains confidentiality of library users records.

Checks in library material and shelves materials in the proper order and place librarian.

Processes library material under the direction of the collection librarian.

Keeps work areas neat.

Assists with ongoing book inventory.

Attends staff meetings to learn all procedures and the changes.

Performs other related duties as required.

Job Requirements

Knowledge: This position requires a basic knowledge of library practices, procedures and techniques; regulations and departmental policies pertaining to library services.

Skills: This position requires skills in word processing, filing and using the library equipment including the online catalogue and automation system. Skills in dealing with people.

Abilities: Position requires ability to learn a variety of procedures; understand the role and the purpose of the library; establish good rapport with library users; pay attention to accuracy; work with interruptions; maintain confidentiality; maintain effective working relationship with fellow employees, supervisors and the public and to communicate effectively.

Education and Experience: The above knowledge, skills, ability are usually acquired through a combination of education and/or experience equivalent to:

- A high school diploma or GED equivalent.
- Library classes or experience working in a library is preferred.
- Strong interest in reading preferred.

Job Performance Standards: Evaluation of this position will be based primarily upon performance of the preceding requirements and duties. Examples of job performance criteria include, but are not limited to, the following:

- Performs assigned duties.
- Meets the objectives of the library as established by the Board
- Competently processes books and other materials.
- Competently serves library users at the circulation desk.
- Properly shelves all library materials.
- Accurately types.
- Keep work areas neat.
- Maintains confidentiality of sensitive information.
- Deals tactfully and courteously with public.
- Observes work hours.
- Demonstrates punctuality.
- Establishes and maintains effective working relationships with fellow employees, supervisors and the public.

Collections Librarian

Sample 1

Position: Collection Librarian

Department: County Library

Accountable To: Library Director

Summary of Work: Maintains the library's collection through cataloging, classifying and processing of books, serials and other library materials. Makes decisions on how the collection can best serve the library users.

Job Characteristics

Nature of Work: This position performs administrative, supervisory and professional duties requiring adherence to standards of accuracy, timeliness, tact and confidentiality. Position requires ability to move and shelve heavy books. Position works varying work schedule and includes some evenings and weekends. Consequence of errors may result in dissatisfied patrons and loss of time to find and correct mistakes.

Personal Contacts: Continual and demanding contact with the public. Coordinates duties with other employees and supervisor to complete tasks.

Supervisions Received: Direction from Library Director.

Essential Functions: Position requires ability to communicate orally and in writing, retrieve and return books to shelves, type, supervise, calculate, read written material, maintain files, operate a computer, operate library machines and equipment. Maintains and applies a thorough knowledge of the library automation system.

Areas of Job Accountability and Performance: Strives to meet the objectives of the library as established by the Board.

Assists and/or organizes library programmes and events. Writes programme grants and or coordinating fundraising for programmes with the Friends of the Library and the Foundation such as the annual reading and discussion series.

Acts as lead worker in the management of library's collection by using the library's online catalogue system, OCLC/WLN and LaserCat databases. Cataloging requires following AACR2 catalogue rules, Dewey Decimal classifications and Library of Congress subjects.

Supervises assistants, volunteers and student workers with technical processing, reclassification, inventory, evaluating gifts, assessing and weeding the collection. Recommends library material purchases.

Collaborates with children's librarian to develop a young adult collection. Serves all library users by assisting with reference questions. Answers the telephone as needed. Works at the circulation desk as assigned. Checks in library material and shelves materials as assistance is needed.

Works as manager of the library's serials. Checks in serials as they are received by mail. Sets up procedures to organize the collection to make it accessible to library users.

Assists the reference librarian with interlibrary loan.

Performs other related duties as required.

Job Requirements

Knowledge: This position require a thorough knowledge of library practices, procedures and techniques; knowledge of classic literature, best sellers lists and reference/information sources, children's literature; knowledge of OCLC/WLN and LaserCat databases, a working knowledge of the laws, regulations and departmental policies pertaining to library services.

Skills: This position requires skills in the use of computers and library equipment; skills in dealing with people.

Abilities: Position requires ability to: work well with library users; supervise assistants and volunteers; complete tasks; pay attention to accuracy; work with interruptions; maintain confidentiality; stay abreast on new procedures affecting library and services; maintain effective working relationships with fellow employees, other agencies and the public; communicate clearly and effectively verbally and in writing.

Education and Experience: The above knowledge, skills, ability are usually acquired through a combination of education and/or experience equivalent to:

- A Bachelor's Degree and three years of experience working in a public library is preferred.
- Current state certification is preferred.
- Strong interest in reading preferred.

Job Performance Standards: Evaluation of this position will be based primarily upon performance of the preceding requirements and duties. Examples of job performance criteria include, but are not limited to, the following:

- Performs assigned duties.

- Meets the objectives of the library as established by the Board
- Competently catalogues, classifies and processes books and other materials.
- Understands tools required to upload MARC records into the online catalogue.
- Competently recommends purchases for young adult collection.
- Effectively assists all library users in the use of the library.
- Maintains confidentiality of sensitive information.
- Maintains accurate and timely records.
- Deals tactfully and courteously with public.
- Observes work hours.
- Keeps work areas neat.
- Demonstrates punctuality.
- Establishes and maintains effective working relationships with fellow employees, supervisors and the public.

Library Director

Sample 1

Class Title: Library Director

Grade: N/A

Accountable To: Library Board of Trustees

Primary Objective of Position: Under general operating standards, plans. organizes, directs, controls and promotes the activities of the City's Library system. Work varies, requiring interpretive judgement: has significant opportunity for discretion and independent action.

Major Areas of Accountability and Performance: (The following are intended to illustrate typical duties not meant to be all inclusive or restrictive,.)

Plans, organizes and manages the services of a city/county library system; establishes goals and measures accomplishments against recognized standards; Studies and makes plans to develop the services of the library or system to meet more effectively present and future community needs, including study of community and area trends and their relation to the library; Advises, consults and confers with the Library Board, other libraries, professionals, officials (at State and local levels), citizens and community groups; supervises and develops procedures, policies and public information and reference service methods used; requisitions supplies, selects books and materials to be purchased, reviews book stock for replacement, repair and discard; Enforces library riles for the protection of library property.

Recruits, selects and trains new personnel; coordinates the continuing training and development of staff members; periodically evaluates the performance of subordinate department heads and supervises the evaluation of other employees;

Prepares speeches and Correspondence Supervises the keeping of records and the preparation of reports, Prepares and presents complex library budgets and adjusters expenditures; Prepares grant applications and seeks funding for operational and improvement programmes; Ensures timely completion of all reports; Works with the Library Board in formulating library procedures, policies, budgets and goals; Acts as Secretary of the Library Board; Actively seeks grants, gifts and other new sources of non-tax funding for the library; Directs a public relations programme to promote and publicize the Library in the community; Supervises the maintenance of the physical plant; Maintains current knowledge of new developments in the library field, *i.e.*, computer technology, library automation and library management; Participates actively in State and National professional organizations.

Initiates plans, develops and implements records and report systems and schedules. Has access to or possesses information restricted to specific persons. Routinely responsible for large amounts of funds. Oversees equipment and facilities requiring care to assure against deterioration. Contacts are varied and continual, requiring a high degree of tact, diplomacy and judgement.

Working Conditions and Physical Requirements: The physical requirements described here are representative of those that must be met by an employee to successfully perform the essential functions of this job. Reasonable accommodations my be made to enable individuals with disabilities to perform the essential functions.

Duties are performed indoors in office environment. Duties require extended periods of standing, walking, sitting, talking or hearing and using hands to finger, handle or feel. Duties require occasional periods of climbing or balancing, pulling/pushing items, lifting/carrying items, keyboarding, reaching with hands and arms, tasting or smelling and stooping, kneeling, crouching, or crawling. Weights up to 50 pounds are encountered. Vision requirements include close vision and ability to adjust focus. Must be able to do math at the algebraic level. Reading materials and verbal instructions require complex interpretation. Hazards are considered minor and controllable, but may include exposure to human error and angry/hostile humans. The noise level is usually moderate. Must be able to transport oneself to work-related meetings, workshops, conferences, etc.

Supervision—Responsibility for Work of Others: Responsible for a large number of professional, clerical and other personnel including volunteers, through subordinate supervisors.

Education, Training and Requirements: A Master's degree in Library Science (MLS) from an A.L.A. accredited institute plus five years of progressively responsible experience in library work, including two years in a supervisory capacity.

Examples of Performance Criteria and Qualifications: Effectively directs and administers the City's library system and programmes;

- Establishes realistic goals and actively works to achieve them;
- Actively and effectively studies the community's needs and actively works to fulfil such needs;

- Effectively supervises, trains and evaluates employees;
- Effectively and tactfully works with and aids community groups, individuals and the public;
- Develops and maintains a level of discipline and working climate in which all personnel are motivated to perform to the best of their abilities;
- Maintains an adequate inventory of books, periodicals and other library stock, within the confines of a budget;
- Maintains an orderly and usable catalogue file, shelving systems and record systems;
- Prepares and presents clear, concise and comprehensive reports as required;
- Effectively and efficiently prepares and administers budgets and grants for the department;
- Maintains and applies thorough knowledge of the principles and practices of modern librarianship and public library administration and continually upgrades, within the confines of a budget.
- Effectively analyzes and develops plans for improving library services;
- Speaks preciely and clearly in public;
- Generates original and innovative thinking formulating and executing library programmes;
- Meets and deals tactfully and effectively with the public;
- Responds appropriately to inquiries and complaints;
- Establishes, maintains and fosters positive and harmonious working relationships with those contacted in the course of work;
- Exercises good judgment, flexibility, creativity and sensitivity in response to changing situations and needs; communicates clearly and concisely, both orally and in writing.

Sample 2

Nature of Work: The position in this class performs administrative and professional library work in managing the County library system.

The tasks performed require the employee to exercise independent judgment and decision making in planning, directing and coordinating all activities of the library including central library headquarters and three branch libraries. Coordinates the activities in the related libraries in contracting school districts, the local community college, veterans home and youth camp. The employee is responsible for planning the long term development of the library programme.

Work is performed under the general policies established by the governing Board of Trustees and reviewed by the Board during an annual performance review. Budgetary guidelines are set by the Board of County Commissioners and the Library Board. Supervision is exercised over a staff of professional, paraprofessional, clerical and other employees in various divisions including technical processing, circulation, reference, extension services, business office and building maintenance.

Contact is maintained by phone in person, or in writing with other county department heads particularly the county attorney, treasurer and clerk and recorder, as well as local city councils. Contact is also maintained with the general public and civic groups in a public relations capacity.

Work is performed in an office environment, but requires the operation of a vehicle to visit branch libraries and attend meetings.

Representative Examples of Work: Only major tasks are identified for most positions; refer to position description for detailed listing of duties.

Plans and directs all phases of the operation of the County library; administers the professional, financial, personnel and business activities.

Confers with and advises division heads on problems-related to the administration of the library services.

Studies methods and makes plans to develop the services of the library to meet more effectively the present and future community needs; establishes programmes and services for the library consistent with community expectations; reviews procedural and operational details for refinements.

Instructs supervisory personnel in general policies and procedures and conducts staff conferences, meetings and training.

Presents written and verbal reports keeping the County Commissioners and the Library Board informed about library operations and services.

Investigates new library techniques and procedures, revises present methods to improve the services; evaluates existing programmes and practices.

Confers with other officials, citizens, clubs and other community organizations, explaining the library system objectives and policies and library services.

Participates in community activities, presenting lectures and talks about the library services.

Prepares and justifies the annual budget estimate; prepares reports to inform the Library Board of activities; submits plans of service for Board review; monitors expenditures; initiates grant requests.

Assists professional staff in the performance of patron service activities as manpower needs require.

Serves as liaison for regional library data base network.

Acts as secretary for the library Board of Trustees.

Performs related work as assigned.

Selection Factors: These factors will be the basis for selecting the most qualified applicants to be interviewed. Applicants selected for employment must satisfactorily demonstrate possession of these factors during and after a prescribed probationary period for continued employment.

Knowledge of:

- the principles, methods and practices of library administration and personnel management.
- library trends, services and equipment.
- community needs and interests in relation to library services.
- reader interest levels and a wide knowledge of books, authors, bibliographies and reference materials.

- cataloguing and classification plans.
- sound methods of management, supervision and training.

Skill in:

- establishing and maintaining effective working relationships with the Library Board, County Commissioners, community leaders, professional groups, subordinates and the public.
- analyzing library needs, evaluating library services and developing library programmes to meet the needs of patrons.
- speaking and writing effectively.
- planning, organizing and directing the work of subordinates.

Ability to:

- obtain a valid Montana driver's license.
- learn and abide by Flathead County library policies and procedures.
- learn and abide by Montana library laws.
- develop budget estimates and prepare statistical reports and summaries.

General Recruitment Indicators (Persons applying for a position in this class should have the following experience and/or training.)

Five years of increasingly responsible administrative library experience including two years in a supervisory capacity and graduation from a college or university with a master's degree in library science; or any equivalent combination of experience and training which indicates possession of the knowledges, skills and abilities listed.

Sample 3

Position: Library Director

Date: October 28,1999

Department: Library

Accountable To: Library Board of Trustees

Summary of Work: This position supervises and administers the delivery of library services to the public and the community, supervises staff and volunteers, prepares budgets and schedules. In addition, this position is responsible for all facilities, equipment and materials. Acts as Coordinator of Sagebrush Federation.

Job Characteristics

Nature of Work: This position involves complex administrative, supervisory and professional duties requiring adherence to professional standards of accuracy, confidentiality, integrity and tact. Regular travel is required.

Personal Contacts: Continual contact with the staff, volunteers and public. Routine contact with the Board, other department heads and other librarians. Occasional contact with the Library Foundation, Friends of the Library and other community organizations.

Supervision Received: Direction from the Board.

Supervision Exercised: Direct supervision of departmental employees and volunteers.

Essential Functions: Position requires ability to plan, implement and evaluate services, communicate orally and in writing, read written material, calculate mathematical figures, maintain files, train staff and volunteers, automate library functions and operate library machines and equipment.

Areas of Job Accountability and Performance

Specific Duties: Develops clear and visionary objectives for accomplishment of evolving library services for the community; prepares and administers the library budgets; keeps informed of new developments in service and information use and applies it to the community; prepares grants for additional funding for special projects; manages and updates automation of the library; selects library materials; selects Library Foundation Memorials as directed; submits vouchers and claims to appropriate funding sources, oversees building and equipment maintenance, including emergency situations; Serves on appropriate committees to represent library services and needs;

prepares reports and statistics as required by the State Library and local government; participates in city government as department head; represents Public Library at all levels of government.

Supervises and trains staff and volunteers; evaluates staff on an annual basis; provides continuing education opportunities for staff, employs and discharges staff as set forth in the union contract; schedules staff, promotes the volunteer programme.

Serves as secretary to the Library Board of Trustees; reports to the Library Board of Trustees, to include but not limited to:

- o recommendations and implementation of policies
- o library issues
- o problem and concerns
- o condition of the Library facilities and equipment;

Provides public relations for the library, including speaking to community groups; determines needs and interests of community for programmes and book selection; and provides programmes and services for community members;

Acts as liaison between the Library Foundation and the Library Board of Trustees; acts as liaison between the Friends of the Library and the Library Board of Trustees;

Prepares and administers the Sagebrush Federation plan of service and budget; provides consultation, assistance and continuing education opportunities to all libraries in the Federation; attends Federation Coordinator meetings and State Library Commission meetings; provides public relations for the Federation; and represents the Sagebrush at all levels of government.

General Duties: Routine librarian duties; assists patrons with their requests; accepts interlibrary loan requests; processes, prepares and repairs books and other materials; maintains a pleasant decor in the library.

Complies with all city and library policies; knowledgeable of union contract provisions, adheres to confidentiality; uses proper phone etiquette, courtesy and appropriate interpersonal communications skills on a routine basis; performs other related duties as requested.

Job Reouirements

Knowledge: This position requires a thorough knowledge of library practices; programmes, procedures and techniques; a working knowledge of the laws, regulations, city policies and library policies pertaining to services, the principles and techniques of budget preparation, personnel management and computer literacy; and a limited knowledge of building maintenance.

Skills: This position requires the use of library equipment, computers and automation equipment. This position must be able to drive.

Abilities: This position requires the ability to work well with people; to plan, direct and regulate library services; to demonstrate initiative; to solve problems; to maintain confidentiality; to stay abreast on new legislation and/or procedures affecting library and services; to prepare accurate reports; to keep the Board informed; to communicate effectively orally and in writing; to follow verbal and written instructions; to establish effective working relationships with staff, volunteers, trustees, public and the community.

Education and Experience

- o Bachelor's degree in related field or bachelor's degree in unrelated field with library science minor or library science endorsement required.
- o Five years library work experience required.
- o Two years administrative and supervisory experience in a library required.
- o Masters of Library Sciences or equivalent preferred.
- o Current state certification is required or must be obtained within 3 years of employment.

Other Requirements: Must have a valid driver's license; must have a personal vehicle and vehicle liability insurance; must be able to travel overnight; must be eligible for coverage by the City insurance carrier; must be bondable, if required.

Job Performance Standards: Evaluation of this position will be based primarily upon performance of the preceding requirements and duties. Examples of job performance criteria include, but are not limited to, the following:

- o Develops and presents goals and objectives
- o Plans, organizes, directs, coordinates and evaluates library functions
- o Establishes and maintains effective working relationships with fellow employees, supervisors, the public and the community
- o Maintains knowledge of accepted practices of library work including ordering, classifying and technical services
- o Studies community needs and actively works to fulfil good public relations and to promote library services
- o Keeps Library Board of Trustees informed on all pertinent issues and submits sound recommendations and polices regarding short and long term needs
- o Carries out Library Board of Tmstees' recommendations and policies
- o Schedules appropriate library hours and staff coverage to meet community needs
- o Works appropriate hours and schedules to supervise and deliver effective library services
- o Prepares, maintains and submits accurate and timely reports and records
- o Develops, organizes and supervises programmes effectively.
- o Shows initiative and resourcefulness
- o Shows flexibility and ability to adjust to change
- o Delegates appropriate authority to staff and volunteers
- o Presents a comprehensive library based on an appropriate mix of library materials

Sample 4

County Library Director Position Description

October, 1999

Position: Library Director

Department: County Library

Accountable To: County Library Board

Summary of Work: This position requires a customer service oriented librarian to direct all programmes, activities and personnel of the library to provide city and county residents with library materials and services to meet their needs. The library director manages and maintains the library facility.

Job Characteristics: Nature of Work: This position performs administrative, supervisory and professional duties requiring adherence to library standards, as well as adhering to standards of accuracy, timeliness, tact and confidentiality. Position works varying work schedule which includes evening and weekends. Position does some travel for meetings and workshops. Consequence of errors may result in dissatisfied library users, employees, board members, city and county officials and possibly a reduction in revenue and dismissal.

Personal Contacts: Continual contact with library employees and the public. Monthly meetings with the library board, city and county officials. Frequent contact with other librarians and salespersons.

Supervision Received: Direction from the County Library Board.

Supervision Exercised: Supervises the library staff including the custodian and the volunteers. Recommends hiring, assigns and disciplines all employees and volunteers in the library. Trains and evaluates all library employees and volunteers.

Essential Functions: Position requires ability to communicate orally and in writing, organize, maintain records, plan and direct services. Requires the ability to oversee budgets, calculate, type, operate computers, library machines and equipment. Maintains a thorough and growing knowledge of the Internet, library automation systems and electronic databases.

Areas of Accountability and Performance: Organizes and directs all library activities according to the County Library Policies to aid the further education and recreation of all people in the Community by providing books, materials, programmes and exhibits.

Advertises for, recommends, assigns and directs the supervision of library employees and volunteers to assure the most efficient use of their time to provide the best service for library users by observing and evaluating employees according to their position description and library users comments.

Prepares, justifies and follows a budget for the Library Board, County Commissioners and the City Council, accounting for all money requested and received following the budgeting, accounting and reporting system of the City Clerk, Montana State Library and Federation.

Attends Library Board meetings to suggest, discuss and promote policies concerning library services, the building, equipment and employees and to act as secretary to the Library Board, taking minutes and keeping all records as required.

Promotes Library services in the community to expand interest and increase contributions through good public relations with individuals, organizations and other librarians by answering correspondence, writing newspaper articles, giving talks, conducting tours, attending meetings and assisting library users and other librarians.

Responsible for managing the activities and staff to achieve a computing environment that serves the libraries' current needs and ensures the development of new services and resources to meet user and staff needs. Provides leadership in designing, maintaining and enhancing the libraries' computing networks and workstations, including the selection of software and equipment for complex systems. Keeps current on new technologies, which may require continuing education and/or certification to operating systems.

Writes grants and coordinates fundraising with Library Friends and Foundation. Travels to out-of-town and/or attends local meetings of professional groups to keep abreast of current techniques and technical advancements, including the Federation meetings and meetings called by the State Library staff and other Library associations.

Serves as Coordinator for the Federation, providing the County Library remains as the headquarters library for the federation. Provides system administration services for the area network of libraries.

This position maintains the online catalogue and automation system to perform at optimum level, making certain the County Library remains as the central site to the network. Plans and organizes training for libraries in the network, recommends policies, continues to work to expand the network, troubleshoots systems, administers installation of upgrades, recommends purchases and implements equipment and software that would improve system and online catalogue. Advocates library services and access to information locally and state wide.

Job Requirements

Knowledge: Considerable knowledge of general library practices and procedures; cataloging, reference, research and bibliographic tools and techniques. Knowledge and experience in technology services. Knowledge of the people of the community and county, their occupations, culture, life styles and interests. Knowledge of personnel principles and practices.

Skills

Managerial Skills: Competency to develop clear and appropriate objectives, plans and procedures in response to programme directives. Competency to use information to evaluate alternatives and select the most appropriate decision. Competency to keep activities organized and operating efficiently.

Financial Skills: Ability to present budgetary and financial information in an organized and understandable manner. Ability to read and understand computer produced accounting statements. Capacity to monitor financial accounts, identify expenditure patterns and take or recommend corrective action.

Interpersonal Skills: Capacity to understand and be sensitive to the needs of individuals. Capacity to interact with others in ways which strengthen and build good feelings. Ability to supervise professional, technical and clerical staff.

Communication Skills: Competency to write effectively in a clear, readable manner with appropriate style, format, organization and grammar. Competency to speak and listen effectively in one-to-one and group situations.

Education and Experience: A Masters of Library Science Degree or four years public library experience or an equivalent of experience indicating an ability to assume responsibilities involved. Rural library experience is desirable.

Physical Demands and Working Conditions: The Library Director must have acceptance of a varying work schedule. Light lifting, stretching and kneeling will be required as shelving books or other projects demand. Standing at the circulation desk for at least two hours at a time is required, as well as sitting at a desk for long periods at a time. The Library Director should work at various hours throughout the month so that he/she works all hours at least once a month. The position requires travel for some meetings and workshops.

Job Performance Standards: Evaluation of this position will be based primarily upon performances of the preceding requirements and duties. Examples of job performance criteria include, but are not limited to, the following:

- Organizes and directs all library activities.
- Oversees the collection management.
- Hires, supervises and evaluates all library employees.
- Prepares, justifies and follows the budget approved by the Library Board
- Attends all Library Board meetings serving as the secretary.
- Promotes and lobbies library service locally and state wide.
- Acts as agent for the Library Foundation.
- Travels to professional meetings that may be sponsored by but not limited to Montana State Library, Federation and Montana Library Association.
- Supervises maintenance and repairs to the Library building, grounds and equipment.
- Recommends to the Library Board the purchase of capital outlay items.

- Serves as the Coordinator for the Federation, planning advisory board meetings, training for librarians and following the plan-of-service set by the advisory board.
- Provides professional services to the area network of libraries in the automated circulation and public online catalogue systems.

Sample 5

Position: Library Director

Department: Public Library

Accountable To: Library Board

Summary of Work: Assesses, selects, purchases, processes and prepares library materials, including appropriate computer hardware and software; assists patrons with reference questions, accessing all appropriate sources, in both paper and electronic formats; researches and prepares annual library budget; maintains and compiles annual library use statistics; responsible for daily operation of a small public library; performs other duties relating to the operation of the library.

Job Characteristics: Nature of work: This position performs administrative and technical duties. Position is involved in managing, organizing and maintaining library materials and services according to established procedures; heavy computer use; assisting patrons effectively; and performing related library duties.

Personal Contacts: Daily contact with the public; other library staff, other town employees; other county and state librarians; library board members.

Supervision Received: Minimal supervision. Guidance as needed.

Supervision Exercised: Supervision of library staff, volunteers.

Essential Functions: Position requires ability to communicate professionally orally and in writing; to use a variety of computer resources, including word-processing, database management and spreadsheet software, as well as library automation systems, electronic information resources and Internet-based resources; to retrieve information, whatever its source or format; to think creatively and problem-solve; read written material.

Areas of Job Accountability and Performance: Serves as secretary for all Library Board meetings; announces, helps plan agendas (with Library Board Chairperson); implements Board policies, procedures and recommendations. Researches, proposes needs of library, including computer software and hardware; composes and prepares all library correspondence; proposes annual library budget; acts as liaison between Library Board and town officials.

Maintains records; writes weekly library column for local newspaper. Controls discretionary spending within annual budget; assists Board with annual budget preparation. Performs other related duties as required.

Job Requirements

Knowledge: This position requires a thorough knowledge of library methods, practices and procedures, including administration, ordering, processing, classification, reference and cataloging.

Skills: This position requires skills in word-processing; Windows 95 and familiarity with computer networking; knowledge of standardized library administration; filing; bookkeeping and the operation of library and office equipment.

Abilities: This position requires the ability to: administer the daily operation of the library; process books and other materials; use computers effectively in a library setting; to prepare and monitor the library budget; to communicate professionally verbally and in writing,; to be dependable, efficient and honest; to establish effective working relationships with employees, the public, other town employees and Library Board.

Education and Experience: The above knowledge, skills and abilities are typically acquired through a combination of experience and education equivalent to a college degree. A Master's degree from an AIA-accredited institution is highly desirable. Experience working with the public is preferred. Prior library experience is also recommended.

Job Performance Standards: Evaluation of this position will be based primarily upon the preceding job description requirements and duties. Examples of job performance standards include but are not limited to the following:

- performs assigned duties;
- adheres to state law influencing the duties and responsibilities of the position;
- maintains accurate records;
- works independently;
- prepares and submits timely reports;
- maintains communication with Library Board on conditions which influence the position;
- displays consideration and cooperation in dealing with the public;
- oversees expenditures of library funds;
- acts as liaison between the public; various federal, state and county agencies;
- establishes effective working relationships with employees, other agencies and professionals, the public and library board.

Sample 6

Position Description: Library Director

General, Purpose : Performs a variety of administrative and supervisory work and complex clerical work in planning, organizing and implementing the programmes and services of the library system.

Supervision Received: Works under the broad policy guidance and direction of the Board of Trustees of the City Library.

Supervision Exercised: Exercises administrative direction over library assistant and volunteer workers.

Essential Duties and Responsibilities: Manages and supervises library operations to achieve goals within available resources; plans and organizes workloads and staff assignments; trains, motivates and evaluates assigned staff; reviews progress and directs changes as needed.

Provides leadership and direction in the development of short and long range library plans; gathers, interprets and prepares data for studies, reports and recommendations; coordinates activities with other libraries and agencies as needed.

Provides professional advice on library issues to library board, commissions, civic groups and the general public.

Communicates official plans, policies and procedures to staff and the general public.

Prepares annual budget requests; assures effective and efficient use of budgeted funds, personnel, materials, facilities and time.

Oversees the selection and general collection of books and other items contained in the library; prepares purchase orders; reviews major selection tools; reviews books, periodicals and collections which are outdated or not used and coordinates removal and disposition.

Oversees inter-library loans and in-house reference work.

Coordinates the library programme with other leisure programmes, other city departments and outside organizations such as the school district, historical society and various community-based groups.

Reviews programme areas, implements changes or new programmes to meet library needs of the community; develops, maintains and implements a library master plan.

Develops and implements policies, procedures and standards for efficient and effective operation and maintenance of library operations. Assures compliance with established policies and procedures.

Promotes interest in library programmes through publicity, programme brochures, cooperation with various community groups and public contacts; speaks before citizens groups, students and other business and civic organizations.

Prepares and administers budget for all areas under library department; orders all new and replacement equipment.

Prepares a variety of reports and maintains necessary operating records.

Maintains liaison with other departments as well as state, local and other public officials.

Answers letters of inquiry and talks with patrons; addresses public and civic organizations which will inform the public of policies, procedures and the availability of facilities for public use. Schedules and runs various special library activities throughout the year, such as book sales, reading programmes, etc.

Peripheral Duties: Performs a variety of miscellaneous duties such as answering phone, running errands, picking up supplies needed for activities and making arrangements for use of library facilities. Maintains confidentiality of records.

Assists staff in the performance of their duties as required.

Minimum Qualifications

Education and experience:

(a) Graduation from high school or GED with some college education desirable and a literacy level commensurate with this educational level.

(b) Two years of employment, community service, or education in library work or related field.

(c) Positive work record in personnel supervision.

Necessary Knowledge, Skills and Abilities:

(a) Thorough knowledge of the principles and practices of modern library systems and programmes; Thorough knowledge of library collection classification and selection techniques; Considerable knowledge of equipment and facilities required in the comprehensive library system; considerable knowledge of community library needs and resources; Working knowledge of the principles and practices of office management, work organization and supervision.

(b) Skill in operation of listed tools and equipment.

(c) Ability to plan, organize, coordinate and implement a comprehensive library system; Ability to coordinate, analyze and utilize a variety of reports and records; Ability to communicate effectively, verbally and in writing; Ability to establish and maintain effective working relationships with employees, supervisors, other agencies and the public. Needs pleasant personality and good grooming habits as to leave a proper impression and good telephone personality.

Special Requirements: Valid state driver's license or ability to obtain one.

Tools and Equipment Used: Library computer system, including work processing and data base management software; calculator; copy and fax machine; phone; automobile.

Physical Demands: The physical demands described here are representative of those that must be met by an employee to successfully perform the essential functions of this job. Reasonable accommodations may be made to enable individuals with disabilities to perform the essential functions.

While performing the duties of this job, the employee is frequently requires to walk, sit and talk or hear. The employee is occasionally required to use hands to finger, handle, feel or operate objects, tools, or controls; and reach with hands and arms. The employee is occasionally required to climb or balance; stoop, kneel, crouch, or crawl. Must be able to tolerate all types of dust.

The employee must occasionally lift and/or move up to 40 pounds. Specific vision abilities required include close vision, distance vision, colour vision, peripheral vision, depth perception and the ability to adjust focus.

Work Environment: The City is an equal opportunity employer. The work environment characteristics described here are representative of those an employee encounters while performing the essential functions of this job. Reasonable accommodations may be made to enable individuals with disabilities to perform the essential functions.

The noise level in the work environment is generally quiet.

Selection Guidelines: Formal application, rating of education and experience; oral interview and reference check; job related tests may be required.

The duties listed above are intended only as illustrations of the various types of work that may be performed. The omission of specific statements of duties does not exclude them from the position if the work is similar, related or logical assignment to the position.

The job description does not constitute an employment agreement between the employer and employee and is subject to change by the employer as the needs of the employer and requirements of the job change.

Sample 7

Position: Director

Programme: Public library

Accountable To: Board of trustees

Summary of Work: This position is responsible for all operational functions of the library including but not limited to: book check out and return, sorting and re-shelving, customer service, inter-library loans, handling of fine notification and revenue, the ordering and purchasing of library books and supplies and the supervision of volunteers and cleaning staffers.

Job Characteristics

Nature of Work: This position performs administrative and customer service duties that require patience and attention to detail. Work is performed primarily in the library with occasional travel requirements. This position performs duties that periodically require working outside of normal business hours. Position is responsible for all petty cash (no more than $100.00 monthly). Confidentiality of patron's reading materials and habits is imperative.

Personal Contacts: This position comes into daily contact with the public in the form of answering questions, assisting with locating materials, etc.

Supervision Received: Instruction is provided by the Board of Trustees on an as needed basis.

Supervision Exercised: This position is responsible for the supervision of volunteers, community service workers and cleaning personnel on an as needed basis.

Essential Functions: This position requires the ability to: communicate effectively orally and in writing; follow verbal and written instructions; establish effective working relationships with fellow employees, supervisors and the public; answer questions patiently; purchase appropriate materials for the library; work with a variety of age levels and interests; handles petty cash; keep a strict level of confidentiality; read fine print; stoops and reach to re-shelve books; lift at least 20 lbs.; calculate; be professional, knowledgeable and courteous when dealing with all library users.

Job Requirements

Knowledge: This position requires a thorough working knowledge of: library management; library patrons reading requirements (recreational, educational, etc.); card catalogue filing system; researching techniques; basic bookkeeping.

Skills: This position requires skills in the us of: computer, typewriter and copier; card catalogue filing system.

Abilities: This position requires the ability to: communicate effectively orally and in writing; follow verbal and written instructions; establish effective working relationships with fellow employees, supervisors and the public; answer questions patiently; complete multiple tasks in a limited amount of time; work with a variety of age levels and interests; keep a strict level of confidentiality; read fine print; stoop and reach to re-shelve books; lift at least 20 lbs.; calculate; be professional knowledgeable and courteous when dealing with all library users.

Education and Experience: The above knowledge, skills and abilities are typically acquired through a combination of education and experience equivalent to:

High School diploma or GED certificate.

One to two years general library experience.

Must be able to become certified by the Montana State Library.

Job Performance Standards: Evaluation of this position will be based primarily upon performance of the preceding requirements and duties. Examples of job performance criteria include, but are not limited to, the following:

Performs assigned duties.

Observes work hours.

Demonstrates punctuality.

Effectively checks books in and out, answers reference questions and re-shelves all returned materials.

Areas of Job Accountability And Performance: Checks books in and out, answers reference questions and reshelves all returned materials.

Responsible for researching inter-library loan requests.

Purchases all library materials (books, videos and audio tapes) for the adult and children's section.

Prepares all library materials for re-shelving.

Files cards in the card catalogue.

Types all book pockets and check out cards.

Does periodic maintenance on books when needed, (i.e. *applying a book cover).*

Loads all new book's and other material's records into the computer.

Send out weekly overdue notices and city court notices on overdue items.

Prepares bill and receipts monthly and presents to the Board of Trustees.

Keeps and prepares all statistical reports.

Keeps accurate daily records of all petty cash and donations that are given to the library.

Prepares the following reports: Financial and Receipt Sheet, Interlibrary reimbursement forms and the Collections Development Policy.

Orders library supplies.

Sorts donated books, changes bulletin board and prepares the monthly article for the newspaper.

Does yearly inventory and periodic collection "weeding."

Attends Federation meetings, the yearly Montana Library Association Conference and any other local library meetings.

Ensures that library materials are appropriate for each age group.

Demonstrates punctuality.

Effectively checks books in and out, answers reference questions and reshelves all return materials.

Maintains accurate and timely records.

Prepares and submits accurate and timely reports.

Deals tactfully and courteously with the public.

Adheres to standards of confidentiality.

Establishes and maintains effective working relationships with fellow employees, supervisors and the public.

Competently purchases all library materials (books, videos and audio tapes) for the adult and children's section.

Sample 8

Position Description

Position Title: Library Director

Supervisor: Public Library Board of Trustees

Job Goal: To operate the Public Library, offering a full range of materials, services and programmes useful to the community and to assure the library is operating in compliance with State accreditation standards.

Job Education and Experience

1. High school diploma or GED certificate.
2. One to two years general library experience.
3. Certification by Montana State Library.

Job Performance Requirements

1. *Certification:* enrollment and completion of the Montana State Library Certification Programme.

2. *Knowledge:* a thorough working knowledge of library management, library patrons requirements, card catalogue filing system, researching techniques, basic bookkeeping and statistics.
3. *Skills:* use of computer, typewriter, copy machine, fax machine and card catalogue filing system.
4. *Abilities:* the ability to communicate effectively orally and in writing; follow verbal and written instructions; establish effective working relations with fellow employees, Library trustees and the public; answer questions patiently; complete multiple tasks in a limited amount of time; work with a variety of age levels and interests; keep a strict level of confidentiality; read fine print; stoop and reach to re-shelve books; lift at least 20 pounds; calculate figures; be professional, knowledgeable and courteous when dealing with all library users.

Job Responsibilities

1. *Managerial:* train staff and volunteers to use good management skills. Supervise staff, community service workers and summer reading programmes.
2. *Customer Service:* deal tactfully and courteously with the public of all age levels, providing their needs in a timely manner. Perform interlibrary loans.
3. *Collection Management:* follow the guiding principles of the collection Development Policy. Organize and maintain materials that fulfil community needs. Keep all items in good repair and eliminate outdated materials. Select new titles and catalogue materials. Pursue the return of overdue items and/or replacement value.
4. *Technology Consultant:* provide patrons with assistance and use of computers and monitor customers' use of computer according to Computer use Policy. Maintain hardware and software, follow the principles of the library's Technology Policy.
5. *Public Relations:* publicize library through newspaper, school personnel, civic groups. Maintain good relations with community. Work with Friends of the Library group

in their meetings and activities. Schedule meeting room for public events within the meeting room policy guidelines. Attend city council meetings when requested by Trustees but not acting as Boards's city council representative.

6. *Bookkeeping and Statistics:* record all financial transactions. Prepare bills for Library Board. Maintain statistics for circulation, use, inventory and file reports.
7. *Secretarial:* take car of mail and correspondence daily. Order supplies. Suggest purchases to Library Board.
8. *Clerical:* act as clerk for Trustees, preparing meeting agendas, recording minutes, giving pertinent information on library issues and budget items.
9. *Lobbyist:* follow and inform Trustees of legislation concerning libraries. Lobby when necessary with public officials.
10. *Professional:* attend continuing education workshops. Network with other librarians.
11. Monitor condition of facility and report needed repairs to authorities. Perform minor maintenance of library equipment, *i.e.* copiers, computers, etc.
12. Other duties as needed or assigned by the Library Board.

Sample 9

Final Draft Approved by Library Trustees

Class Title: Library Director

Accountable To: Library Trustees

Primary Objective of Position: Under the general direction of the Library Trustees, works collaboratively with other Library staff members to deliver professional quality library service to the public. Has primary responsibility for all Library services, resources and staff. Integrates Library services with the Library's mission, Strategic Plan and objectives. Is responsible for the maintenance and operation of the Library's automated systems, including circulation (Dynix), network internet connection (Windows NT) and the Library's individual computers, terminals and printers. Supervises cataloging for books and assures quality control for all bibliographic and related records in the Library's catalogue system (Dynix). Plans and administers online access to internal resources (CD-ROM) and external resources (OCLC/InfoTrac/iPage). As a member of the Library staff is required to keep abreast of all Library activities and priorities, with particular focus on how these priorities might affect responsibilities and activities of the Library. Performs all routine library functions including book and periodical shelving.

Major Areas of Accountability and Performance: With the Library Trustees leads the short and long range planning activities of the Library, including new or changed services and budgetary needs. Coordinates this planning with the County's annual and long range planning efforts.

Manages all Library operations, including book and journal collections, automation and information technology, bookmobile, reference and library instruction, budget and facilities, through initiative, coordination and collaboration.

Coordinates and supervises the work of the Library staff, including training, monitoring, evaluating, redirecting and mentoring for growth. The Library staff presently includes five full time employees, two substitutes, the Director of the Adult Learning Centre and a varying number of volunteers.

With the staff and print and technology vendors, assures optimal materials (book, periodical and electronic) selection, development and maintenance. Keeps current with relevant review literature, recommends appropriate library materials and monitors the materials budget.

In collaboration with the staff, works to assure optimal bookmobile services to the rural residents of the county.

Provides back-up staffing of the Library, as needed; participates in a rotating work schedule.

Maintains awareness of trends in public library service and other changes which may indicate new or changed Library collections and services.

Supports overall Library operations and services through projects and other duties as appropriate and assigned. Actively supports Library colleagues, Library service goals and the Library's mission.

As possible, participates in statewide, regional and national activities of the library profession.

Supervision—Responsibility for the Work of Others: Supervises staff, volunteers, work study students, community service workers and summer youth workers, including assigning work, training, monitoring and evaluating assigned work.

Education, Training and Experience Requirements: Masters of Science in Library Science (MSLS) and four years (minimum) of experience in an automated library preferred, including a very high familiarity with the use and management of computerized library resources in a networked environment; affinity for cooperation and collaboration; good interpersonal, verbal and written skills important; service orientation essential; comfort with a varied pace, overlapping tasks, details and change.

Examples of Performance Criteria and Qualifications: Effectively meets the public and assists in the effective use of library and bookmobile resources.

Maintains collaborative working relationships with fellow employees, the Board of Trustees and the governing authority.

Maintains a cordial and professional relationship with the public.

Provides short and long range planning for the Library, both programmematic and budgetary.

Determines focus, policies and priorities for the Library's services.

Determines focus, policies and priorities for collection development, regardless of format (print, microform, electronic, journal).

Supports overall Library operations and services through projects, training and other duties as appropriate and assigned.

Opens the Library building and prepares it for each day's use.

At library closing times, correctly shuts down all equipment including computers, secures the building and assures lock-up.

Examples of Performance Criteria and Qualifications: *Automation.*

Installs, maintains and documents data/video/ telecommunications cable network.

Installs and maintains data communication equipment in network hubs and computers.

Oversees installation and maintenance of voice communications equipment.

Organizes, maintains and documents the microcomputer and network hardware locations and configurations, including physical organization, operating procedures, safety standards, parts inventories and hardware purchasing.

Installs, maintains and repairs library microcomputer and printer equipment.

Maintains a filing and documentation system, including original equipment and installation documentation, equipment and wiring installation and maintenance procedures and equipment inventory.

Maintains and performs regular periodic backup of data on network and circulation computer systems.

Performs all system administration functions for voice and circulation systems and multi-user public access computer systems.

Maintains network information systems, performs network system administration and installs and configures software related to other library job functions.

Maintains documentation for and trains staff involved in, computer and voice system use and administration. Provides complex problem resolution for these systems.

Recommends and supervises contractor and subcontractors and ensures their compliance with work standards and policies and assists in the completion of specific tasks.

Assists patrons and staff with hardware and software related problems.

Communicates with vendors and manufacturers as necessary.

Sample 10

Job Title: Library Director

Current Employee

Supervision: Under the general supervision of the Library Board of Trustees and City Manager as a Department Head.

Min/Max Base Salary: ____________ FTE:__________

Anniversary Date:________________ Employee Signature:

____

Position Overview: The Library Director performs professional library functions requiring specialized knowledge and expertise in all areas of public library services and library administration. This position focuses on management of all departments within the library, policy and collection development, community outreach, reference responsibilities and all budgetary considerations. The Library Director acknowledges and accepts the Library's Code of Service, respects the Library's confidentiality laws and maintains the integrity of the Lewistown Public Library, statewide public library standards, local policies and procedures and state law.

Principle Priorities: Duties may be modified by the Library Board of Trustees.

- Aspires to help patrons to become lifelong library users by introducing them to the wealth of library resources and enables them to use library services effectively.
- Assists patrons in locating needed resources in all formats and provides assistance for Internet usage and computer programmes within the Library.
- Provides Reader Advisory and basic instruction for all ages, as requested, for print materials, Internet usage and computer programmes.
- Sustains the dignity of patrons by giving them correct, non-judgmental and complete responses to their informational needs. Provides help where needed and respects patron's right to browse and maintain's all patrons rights as stated in policies.

- Formally and informally assesses the community regularly to identify community needs and preferences.
- Develops and promotes the services of the Library to meet effectively present and future community needs.
- Plans, organizes, oversees and manages all the services of the Library; including (not exclusively) building management, collection management, Interlibrary Loan transactions, technical processing, public services, youth services and outreach services throughout the library.
- Keeps Library Board and City Manager informed as to project progression, library needs and outcomes.
- Collects data and compiles reports as requested by the Board and other agencies.
- Prepares for and holds monthly library board meetings, keeps board members apprised of current happenings in library profession and to matters related to library operation.
- Researches, drafts and recommends library policies to the Library Board and implements all Library policy as determined by the Library Board of Trustees.
- Handles monetary payments for fines, donations, ILL, etc. Oversees accounting of such monetary matters for the Library, works with Finance Officer of the City on budgetary matters regularly.
- Prepares the annual budget request and monitors its implementation; prepares and submits claims for Library needs.
- Oversees Library endowment activity and solicits donations for the Library, develops and oversees fundraising or grants as needed and appropriate.
- Conducts regular staff meetings.
- Maintains and manages all technological equipment requiring servicing and accountability within the library, assures training for other staff in the use of this equipment.
- Recruits, interviews, hire, supervises, evaluates & recommends termination of all Library staff. Ensures

ongoing training opportunities for all staff and encourages staff development.

- Maintains a neat, clean, functional and inviting library. Provides a welcoming and safe atmosphere for staff and the public; provides and directs safety training to prevent injury, equipment malfunctions and poor public service.
- Designs, develops and implements library marketing promotions.
- Enforces and develops library rules for the protection of library patrons and property.
- Interacts with customers and staff in a courteous and professional manner and attempts to defuse and/or resolve potentially volatile or sensitive situations to ensure quality customer service and effectively deals with all patron complaints & disturbances.
- Performs supervisory and professional duties requiring adherence to standards of accuracy, timeliness, tact and confidentiality.
- Consults with peers on library matters, this may include staff meetings, workshops, Wired Montana listserve, other library listserves, professional gatherings and other resources.
- Stays informed of trends and needed skills through professional reading and continuing education opportunities. Keeps current on new library materials, techniques and technologies.
- Serves the library profession through involvement at the local, state & regional levels with professional organizations.
- Participates in continuing education programmes related to library services and pursues Montana Library Certification.
- Other duties as assigned by the Library Board and City Manager and as approved by the Library Board.

Supervision: Under general supervision of the Library Board of Trustees and the City Manager as a Department Head.

Responsibility for Work of Others: Supervises all Library Staff and volunteers.

Knowledge, Skills and Abilities: Masters in Library or Information Science degree or equivalent Masters Degree, supplemented by course work in library science, literature or related topics is preferred; Required: a Bachelor's Degree with some course work in library science; 5 years progressively responsible work experience in a library environment, including a minimum of one year administrative or supervisory experience. Must earn and maintain MT State Library Certification.

Essential Skills/Abilities: Must demonstrate strong leadership and management abilities; demonstrate a good knowledge and appreciation of children's and adult literature, audiovisual materials, computer resources and other materials that constitute a balanced, relevant library collection; have a good knowledge of reference materials and other library resources which may serve the needs of the community; demonstrates good interpersonal skills in meeting with staff and community members of all ages; demonstrates good active listening skills. Must be an effective and capable public speaker.

Must be able to conduct diverse library programmes with sensitivity to the various needs of the audience and with age appropriate materials and activities. A good working knowledge of library standards and rules such as USMARC and AACR2 is essential. Must be familiar with library tools for evaluating, acquiring and maintaining library collections.

Must know how to use Online Public Access Catalogue, electronic resources and other information technology sources to meet typical library needs. Must demonstrate the ability to conduct a reference interview and be able to answer reference questions with authority and tenacity to meet patron needs. Must have skills in operating personal computers, automated information databases, database creation, word processing, spreadsheets and electronic software. A working knowledge of office procedures is desirable. Must possess a valid Montana Operator's License.

The position requires a commitment to service excellence; the ability to see the big picture of the Library; the ability to work well with others in a team; the ability to provide leadership and plan, prioritize and focus on what is critical; a commitment to lifelong learning; recognition of the value of professional networking; and the ability to remain flexible and positive in a time of continuing change.

Working Conditions and Physical Demands: Physical requirements include ability to move around the facility, walk, sit, bend, climb, kneel, carry and stoop; Ability to use hand and finger motion with enough manual dexterity to use computers and handle library items; Lift up to 25#, or greater with assistance; and perform other efforts as identified with normal library work; must have the ability to communicate with patrons effectively; having the ability to talk with clarity and be able to listen to patrons accurately; Must have specific vision abilities (adjusted) that include close and distance vision with good depth perception; reasonable accommodations may be available; Typing ability and computer skills are essential. Duties are performed in surroundings where undesirable physical conditions and hazards are minor and controllable.

Head Librarian

Sample 1

Position: Head librarian

Accountability: Library board of trustees

Summary of Work: Under the policy guidance and direction of the board, the Head Librarian shall perform the administrative, supervisory and professional work in planning and delivering library services.

Job Characteristics

Nature of Work: Planning and coordinating activities related to library operation

Personal Contact: Frequent contact with public, maintains contact with other departments and professional groups, attends and records minutes from monthly board meetings

Supervision Received: Monthly direction will be given from the board

Supervision Exercised: Daily coordination of duties with library staff and volunteers

Areas of Job Accountability and Performance

- Must have knowledge in and be able to operate a Computer System
- Oversees the daily operation of the library
- Selects circulation, reference and periodical materials
- Prepares preliminary budget, financial and activity reports and presents such information to the board
- Hires, trains, schedules and supervises staff
- Classifies and catalogues library materials
- Shares daily circulation duties
- Maintains employee records
- Determines books and materials to be mended or discarded
- Maintains membership in professional organizations
- Remains informed concerning library-related issues
- Answers public inquires and prepares press releases
- Assists in the activities of the Board
- Communicates with civic groups and elected officials regarding library issues
- Writes grant proposals
- Plans and develops Summer reading programmes
- Performs other related duties as required

Education and Experience

The above knowledge, skills and abilities are typically acquired through a combination of educations and experience equivalent to a masters of Library Science degree, five years training in library services and or a combination of both.

Job Performance Standards: Evaluation of this position will be based primarily upon the preceding job description requirements and duties. Examples of job performance criteria include the following:

- Provides well-rounded library services within budgetary constraints

- Performs assigned duties
- Organizes and supervises library programmes and services effectively
- Promotes library services
- Executes supervisory duties
- Provides information and assistance to the Board of Trustees
- remains informed concerning contemporary library issues
- Maintains accurate records, prepares and submits accurate reports
- Operates within approved budget
- Observes work hours
- Demonstrates punctuality
- Deals tactfully with the public and displays a commitment to public service
- Establishes and maintains effective working relationships with fellow employee, supervisors and the public
- Demonstrates the proper dress for library employees

Library Assistant

Sample 1

Position Description: Library Assistant - City Library

General Purpose: Performs a variety of routine clerical and manual work in circulating and processing library materials and providing services to library patrons.

Supervision Received: Works under the close supervision of a librarian director.

Supervision Exercised: May exercise limited supervision over library aides, or part-time volunteers.

Essential Duties and Responsibilities: Checks library materials in and out.

Performs routine maintenance on books and other materials, reviews books, periodicals and collections which are outdated or not used and coordinates removal and disposition.

Files cards and inputs data into computer.

Answers telephone calls and provides information or otherwise assists or refers patrons as appropriate.

Assists in maintaining library collections and facilities.

Processes inter-library loans and in house reference work.

Performs a variety of miscellaneous duties such as answering phone, running errands, picking up supplies needed for activities. Maintains confidentiality of records.

Peripheral Duties: Conducts tours of library facilities for various educational or civic groups and interested individuals.

Assists patrons in the selection of library materials and provides reference guidance.

Desired Minimum Qualifications

Education and Experience:

(a) Graduation from high school or GED with a literacy level commensurate with this level of education.

(b) Some knowledge of the principles and practices of modern library systems and programmes; Some knowledge of library circulation or processing techniques; Working knowledge of library classification systems; Working knowledge of basic office procedures.

(c) Skill in operation of listed tools and equipment.

(d) Ability to accurately maintain library filling systems; Ability to orally communicate effectively; Ability to establish and maintain effective working relationships with patrons. Needs pleasant personality, good grooming and dress habits as to leave a proper impression on patrons and a good telephone personality.

Special Requirements: Valid state driver's license or ability to obtain one.

Tools and Equipment Used: Library computer system; calculator; copy and fax machine; phone; automobile.

Physical Demands: The physical demands described here are representative of those that must be met by an employee to successfully perform the essential functions of this job. Reasonable accommodations may be made to enable individuals with disabilities to perform the essential functions.

While performing the duties of this job, the employee is frequently required to walk, sit and talk or hear. The employee is occasionally required to use hands to finger, handle, feel or operate objects, tools, or controls; and reach with hands and arms. The employee is occasionally required to climb or balance, stoop, kneel, crouch, or crawl. Must be able to tolerate all types of dust.

The employee must occasionally lift and/or move up to 40 pounds. Specific vision abilities required by this job include close vision, distance vision, colour vision, peripheral vision, depth perception and the ability to adjust focus.

Work Environment: The work environment characteristics described here are representative of those an employee encounters while performing the essential functions of this job. Reasonable accommodations may be made to enable individual with disabilities to perform the essential functions.

The noise level in the work environment is generally quiet.

Selection Guidelines: The City is an equal opportunity employer.

Formal application, rating of education and experience; oral interview and reference check; job related tests may be required.

The duties listed above are intended only as illustrations of the various types of work that may be performed. The omission of the specific statements of duties does not exclude them from the position if the work is similar, related or a logical assignment to the position.

The job description does not constitute an employment agreement between the employer and employee and is subject to change by the employer as the needs of the employer and requirements of the job change.

Sample 2

Final Draft Approved by Library Trustees

Class Title: Library System Operator II - Administration

Accountable To: Library Director

Primary Objective of Position: Under the general direction of the Library Director, works collaboratively with other library staff members to deliver professional quality library service to the public. Has primary responsibility for general and specialized public and reference service utilizing printed and computerized tools. Has special responsibility for the Dynix electronic circulation and book order systems. Shares, with the Library Director, responsibility for the selection of books, collection development and the selection of other relevant information resources in all formats, including the internet. As a member of the Library staff is required to keep abreast of all Library activities and priorities, with particular focus on how these priorities might affect responsibilities and activities within own position. Performs all routine library functions including book and periodical shelving.

Major Areas of Accountability and Performance

- Works collaboratively with other library staff members to coordinate circulation, reference and interlibrary loan work in a rotating schedule.
- In collaboration with the rest of the staff provides general and specialized reference and readers advisory service, library orientation and instruction to the general public and devises search strategies using information resources including the internet, WLN and the book and periodical collections of the library.
- In the absence of the Library Director, can assume operational responsibility for the Library's daily operations.
- Places and tracks orders for books, periodical subscriptions, supplies and other Library receivables, using the applicable Library computer systems and/or manual records.
- Monitors, orders and dispenses all Library supplies. Handles all vendor communications, including Central Supply. Oversees daily mail distribution, including overdue notices and bills from the Library's automated circulation system.

- Performs routine updating functions of the Library's Dynix circulation records.
- Collects and provides statistical reports in areas of responsibility.
- Supports overall Library operations and services through projects and other duties as appropriate and assigned. Actively supports Library colleagues, Library service goals and the Library's mission.
- As possible, participates in state wide and regional and national activities of the library profession.

Supervision—Responsibility for the Work of Others: Supervises as assigned staff, volunteers, work study students, community service workers and summer youth workers, including assigning work, training, monitoring and evaluating assigned work.

Education, Training and Experience Requirements: Bachelor's Degree or two years (minimum) of experience in an automated library preferred, including familiarity with use of computerized library resources; affinity for cooperation and collaboration; good interpersonal, verbal and written skills important; service orientation essential; comfort with a varied pace, overlapping tasks, details and change.

Examples of Performance Criteria and Qualifications: Effectively meets the public and assists in the effective use of library resources.

Maintains collaborative working relationships with fellow employees.

Maintains a cordial and professional relationship with the public.

Within the parameters of position responsibilities, proposes new or changed policies and procedures to accomplish own responsibilities, related operations and Library mission.

Supports overall Library operations and services through projects, training and other duties as appropriate and assigned.

Opens the Library building and prepares it for each day's use.

At library closing times, correctly shuts down all equipment including computers, secures the building and assures lock-up.

Sample 3

Final Draft Approved by Library Trustees

Class Title: Library System Operator II - Bookmobile

Accountable To: Library Director

Primary Objective of Position: Under the general direction of the Library Director, works collaboratively with other Library staff members to deliver professional quality library service to the public. Has primary responsibility for the Library's graphic designs and world wide web pages. Has special responsibility for service to bookmobile patrons. Plans routes and schedules.

Determines the length and location of service stops. Shares with the Library Director responsibility for the selection of bookmobile books and other relevant information resources in all formats, including the internet. As a member of the Library staff is required to keep abreast of all Library activities and priorities, with particular focus on how these priorities might affect responsibilities and activities within own position. Performs all routine library functions including book and periodical shelving.

Major Areas of Accountability and Performance

- Works collaboratively with other Library staff members to plan, organize and coordinate a comprehensive graphics and web programme promoting the Library. Is responsible for planning the operation of the bookmobile service and operating bookmobile trips on a rotating schedule.
- In collaboration with the rest of the Library staff provides general and specialized reference and readers advisory service, library orientation, programmemeing and instruction specifically for bookmobile patrons. Devises search strategies to accommodate bookmobile patrons using information resources, including the internet, WLN and the book and periodical collections of the Library.

- Is responsible for the safe operation of the bookmobile and the personal safety of each bookmobile patron on each trip.
- Is responsible for routine record keeping and maintenance of the bookmobile.
- Collects and provides statistical reports in areas of responsibility.
- In the absence of the Library Director, can assume operational responsibility for the Library's daily operations.
- Monitors, selects from the Library's collections and dispenses library materials used on weekly bookmobile trips. Handles in a timely fashion all patron requests for materials.
- Performs routine updating functions of the Library's Dynix circulation records. Oversees creation of overdue notices and bills from the Dynix automated circulation system.
- Supports overall Library operations and services through projects and other duties as appropriate and assigned. Actively supports Library colleagues, Library service goals and the Library's mission.
- As possible, participates in state-wide, regional and national activities of the library profession.

Supervision—Responsibility for the Work of Others: Supervises as assigned staff, volunteers, work study students, community service workers and summer youth workers, including assigning work, training, monitoring and evaluating assigned work.

Education, Training and Experience Requirements: Bachelor's Degree or two years (minimum) of experience in an automated library preferred, including familiarity with use of computerized library resources; affinity for cooperation and collaboration; good interpersonal, verbal and written skills important; service orientation essential; comfort with a varied pace, overlapping tasks, details and change. Class B1 drivers license required.

Examples of Performance Criteria and Qualifications: Effectively meets the public and assists in the effective use of library and bookmobile resources.

Maintains collaborative working relationships with fellow employees.

Maintains a cordial and professional relationship with the public.

Within the parameters of position responsibilities, proposes new or changed policies and procedures to accomplish own responsibilities, related operations and the Library's mission.

Supports overall Library operations and services through projects, training and other duties as appropriate and assigned.

Opens the Library building and prepares it for each day's use.

Operates the bookmobile in a safe, well maintained and prudent manner.

At library closing times, correctly shuts down all equipment including computers, secures the building and assures lock-up.

Sample 4

Final Draft Approved by Library Trustees

Class Title: Library System Operator II - Public Services
Accountable To: Library Director

Primary Objective of Position: Under the general direction of the Library Director, works collaboratively with other library staff members to deliver professional quality library service to the public. Has primary responsibility for general and specialized public and reference service utilizing printed and computerized tools. Has special responsibility for the public services and interlibrary loan operations of the Library.

Shares with the Library Director responsibility for short and long range planning for library services, resources and staff. Shares with the Library Director the coordination of library operations, including book and journal collections, information technology, reference and library promotion and instruction, budget and facilities, through initiative, coordination and delegation. As a member of the Library staff is required to keep abreast of all Library activities and priorities, with particular focus on how these priorities might affect responsibilities and activities within own position. Performs all routine library functions including book and periodical shelving.

Major Areas of Accountability And Performance

- Works collaboratively with other library staff members to coordinate circulation, reference and interlibrary lending and borrowing through the WLN resource sharing system on a rotating schedule.
- In collaboration with the rest of the staff provides general and specialized reference and readers advisory service, library orientation and instruction to the general public, which may include more than half of each work day on the main floor of the Library interacting with library users. Will at all times be able to devise search strategies to meet patron needs using information resources including the internet, WLN and the book and periodical collections of the library.
- In the absence of the Library Director, can assume operational responsibility for the Library's daily operations.
- Assures that the Library functions smoothly on a day-to-day basis.
- Creates reference guides and other reference self-help and training materials.
- Creates item records in Library's Dynix catalogue and barcoded links to books.
- Performs routine updating functions of the Library's Dynix circulation records.
- Collects and provides statistical reports in areas of responsibility.
- Supports overall Library operations and services through projects and other duties as appropriate and assigned. Actively supports Library colleagues, Library service goals and the Library's mission.

- As possible, participates in state wide and regional and national activities of the library profession.

Supervision—Responsibility for the Work of Others: Supervises as assigned staff, volunteers, work study students, community service workers and summer youth workers including assigning work, training, monitoring and evaluating assigned work.

Education, Training and Experience Requirements: Bachelor's Degree or two years (minimum) of experience in an automated library preferred, including familiarity with use of computerized library resources; affinity for cooperation and collaboration; good interpersonal, verbal and written skills important; service orientation essential; comfort with a varied pace, overlapping tasks, details and change.

Examples of Performance Criteria and Qualifications: Effectively meets the public and assists in the effective use of library resources.

Maintains collaborative working relationships with fellow employees. Maintains a cordial and professional relationship with the public.

Within the parameters of position responsibilities, proposes new or changed policies and procedures to accomplish own responsibilities, related operations and Library mission.

Supports overall Library operations and services through projects, training and other duties as appropriate and assigned.

Opens the Library building and prepares it for each day's use.

At library closing times, correctly shuts down all equipment including computers, secures the building and assures lock-up.

Sample 5

Job Title: Library Assistant I

Supervision: Under the general supervision of the Library Director

Min/Max Base Salary:

Position Overview: A Library Assistant I provides assistance with library functions in offering quality library services to the public. This position focuses on shelving, technical processing assistance and general assistance duties. The Library Assistant I will acknowledge and accept the Library's Code of Service, respect the Library's confidentiality laws and maintain the integrity of the Lewistown Public Library.

Principle Job Priorities (not all inclusive and may be modified at anytime):

General:

- Aspires to help patrons to become lifelong library users by introducing them to the wealth of library resources and enables them to use library services effectively.
- Assists patrons in locating needed resources (general) or referring them to other staff for assistance.
- May provide general assistance for Internet usage and computer programmes within the Library.
- Sustains the dignity of patrons by giving them correct, non-judgmental and complete responses to their informational needs. Provides help where needed and respects patron's right to browse.
- Consults with peers on library matters.
- Keeps Director informed as to project progression, needs and outcomes.
- Collects data and compiles reports as requested.
- May assist in minor maintenance and manages technological equipment (photocopier, printers, AV equipment, computers and reader/printer) requiring minimal servicing and accountability within the library. May handle monetary payments for fines, donations, ILL, etc.
- Enforces library rules for the protection of library patrons and property.
- Helps to maintain a neat, clean, functional and inviting library. Provides a welcoming and safe atmosphere.
- May participate in circulation tasks, which may include checkouts, record keeping, opening and closing routines,

reserves, sorting mail and other tasks associated with circulating materials.

- Assists with library promotion and services as assigned.
- May assist the public, on the phone or in person, on the use, availability and status of library materials.
- Interacts with customers and staff in a courteous and professional manner and refers potentially volatile or sensitive situations to other staff ensure quality customer service.
- Performs duties with adherence to library standards of accuracy, timeliness, tact and confidentiality.

Specific Priorities: (may be modified at anytime)

Shelf Maintenance Responsibilities:

- Assists with shelving library materials.
- May assist with shelf organization, arrangements and shelf maintenance in all areas of the library.
- Maintains shelf and book cleanliness.
- Keeps Director informed as to needs and recommendations.

Technical Processing Responsibilities: Under supervision of *Library Assistant III -Technical Services.*

- Assists in preparing library materials for processing and making them shelf ready.
- Assists in repairs of questionable quality or broken audio and visual cassettes.
- Assists in maintaining library materials, *i.e.* mending and repairs
- Assists in de-processing discarded library materials.

Other Assigned Duties may include:

- Assisting with Youth Services activities and programmes.
- Assisting with Outreach programmes.
- Simple maintenance and manual tasks.
- Other duties as assigned.

Supervision: Under direct supervision of the Library Director, but may be directed in certain tasks by other library staff.

Responsibility for Work of Others: None.

Knowledge, Skills and Abilities: High School diploma or GED is required. A desire to work with the public is essential. Computer knowledge and skills is desirable.

Must be willing to learn or know how to use Online Public Access Catalogue, electronic resources and other information technology sources to meet typical library needs; must feel comfortable referring inquiries to another Library Assistant. A working knowledge of office procedures is desirable. The position requires a commitment to service excellence; the ability to work well with others in a team; and the ability to remain flexible and positive in a time of continuing change.

Working Conditions and Physical Demands: Physical requirements include ability to move around the facility, walk, sit, bend, climb, kneel, stoop, carry; Ability to use hand and finger motion with enough manual dexterity to use computers and handle library items; Lift up to 25#, or greater with assistance; and perform other efforts such as pushing a loaded book cart as identified with normal library work; must have the ability to communicate with patrons effectively; having the ability to talk with clarity and be able to listen to patrons accurately; Must have specific vision abilities (adjusted) that include close and distance vision with good depth perception; reasonable accommodations may be available; Typing ability and computer skills desirable.

Duties are performed in surroundings where undesirable physical conditions and hazards are minor and controllable.

Sample 6

Job Title: Library Assistant II

Current Employee

Supervision: Under the general supervision of the Library Director

Min/Max Base Salary: ____________ FTE:__________

Anniversary Date:______________ Employee Signature:

____

Position Overview: A Library Assistant II performs professional library functions requiring general knowledge in all areas of public library services. This position focuses on shelf management, technical processing and general assistance duties. The Library Assistant II acknowledges and accepts the Library's Code of Service, respects the Library's confidentiality laws and maintains the integrity of the Lewistown Public Library.

Principle Job Priorities (not all inclusive and may be modified at anytime):

General:

- Aspires to help patrons to become lifelong library users by introducing them to the wealth of library resources and enables them to use library services effectively.
- Assists patrons in locating needed resources in all formats and provides assistance for Internet usage and computer programmes within the Library.
- Provides Reader Advisory and basic instruction for all ages, as requested, for print materials, Internet usage and computer programmes.
- Sustains the dignity of patrons by giving them correct, non-judgmental and complete responses to their informational needs. Provides help where needed and respects patron's right to browse.
- Interprets and applies typical library search strategies.
- Informally assesses the community regularly to identify community needs and preferences.
- Composes bibliographies, book reviews and press releases as requested.
- Consults with peers on library matters, this may include staff meetings, workshops, Wired Montana listserve, other library listserves, professional gatherings and other resources.
- Keeps current on new library materials and technologies.
- Prepares correspondence/documentation on procedural or informational matters as needed or requested.

- Keeps Director informed as to project progression, needs and outcomes.
- Collects data and compiles reports as requested.
- Maintains and manages technological equipment (photocopier, printers, AV equipment, computers and reader/printer) requiring minimal servicing and accountability within the library, may train other staff on the use of this equipment as requested.
- Handles monetary payments for fines, donations, ILL, etc.
- Enforces library rules for the protection of library patrons and property.
- Helps to maintain a neat, clean, functional and inviting library. Provides a welcoming and safe atmosphere.
- Participates in circulation tasks, which may include checkouts, record keeping, opening and closing routines, reserves, sorting mail and other tasks associated with circulating materials.
- Plans, implements and follows through with procedural and informational duties and assists with library promotion and services as assigned.
- Assists the public, on the phone or in person, on the use, availability and status of library materials.
- Interacts with customers and staff in a courteous and professional manner and attempts to defuse and/or resolve potentially volatile or sensitive situations to ensure quality customer service.
- Recommends books and other materials to be purchased for the collection.
- Performs supervisory and professional duties requiring adherence to standards of accuracy, timeliness, tact and confidentiality.
- Participates in continuing education programmes related to library services and pursues Montana Library Certification.

Current Specific Priorities: (may be modified at anytime)

Shelf Management Responsibilities:

- Shelves all library materials.
- Scrutinizes shelf organization, arrangements and shelf maintenance in all areas of the library.
- Informs staff of any shelving changes.
- May oversee and/or train volunteers who dust shelves and wash books.
- Keeps Director informed as to needs and recommendations.

Technical Processing Responsibilities: Under supervision of *Library Assistant III -Technical Services.*

- Prepares library materials for processing and makes them shelf ready.
- Reviews and repairs questionable quality or broken audio and visual cassettes.
- Maintains library materials, *i.e.* mending and repairs
- De-processes discarded library materials.

Other Assigned Duties may include:

- Serving as a backup person for youth services and circulation.
- Assisting with Youth Services activities and programmes.
- Assisting with Outreach programmes.
- Simple maintenance and manual tasks.
- Managing and preparing library displays.
- Managing the pet animals needs and care.
- Other duties as assigned.

Supervision: Under general supervision of the Library Director, but may be directed in certain tasks by other library staff.

Responsibility for Work of Others: May oversee volunteers or community workers as appropriate.

Knowledge, Skills and Abilities: High School diploma or GED is required. Some college coursework is preferred. Two years of library experience is required. A desire to work with the public is essential. Computer knowledge and skills is essential. A basic knowledge of MARC and ACCR2 is preferred.

Must know how to use Online Public Access Catalogue, electronic resources and other information technology sources to meet typical library needs; must be able to answer general reference questions with authority and tenacity to meet patron needs or feel comfortable referring to another Library Assistant. A working knowledge of office procedures is desirable. The position requires a commitment to service excellence; the ability to see the big picture of the Library; the ability to work well with others in a team; the ability to provide leadership and plan, prioritize and focus on what is critical; commitment to lifelong learning; recognition of the value of professional networking; and the ability to remain flexible and positive in a time of continuing change.

Working Conditions and Physical Demands: Physical requirements include ability to move around the facility, walk, sit, bend, climb, kneel, stoop, carry and stoop; Ability to use hand and finger motion with enough manual dexterity to use computers and handle library items; Lift up to 25#, or greater with assistance; and perform other efforts as identified with normal library work; must have the ability to communicate with patrons effectively; having the ability to talk with clarity and be able to listen to patrons accurately; Must have specific vision abilities (adjusted) that include close and distance vision with good depth perception; reasonable accommodations may be available; Typing ability and computer skills are essential.

Duties are performed in surroundings where undesirable physical conditions and hazards are minor and controllable.

Sample 7

Job Title: Library Assistant III - Public Services (Collection Development, Community Outreach and Reference)

Current Employee

Supervision: Under the general supervision of the Library Director

Min/Max Base Salary: ____________ FTE:__________

Anniversary Date:______________ Employee Signature:

____

Position Overview: A Library Assistant III - Public Services performs professional library functions requiring specialized knowledge and expertise in all areas of public library services. This position focuses on collection development, community outreach and reference duties. The Library Assistant III acknowledges and accepts the Library's Code of Service, respects the Library's confidentiality laws and maintains the integrity of the Lewistown Public Library.

Principle Priorities: Duties may be assigned or modified by Director.

General:

- Aspires to help patrons to become lifelong library users by introducing them to the wealth of library resources and enables them to use library services effectively.
- Assists patrons in locating needed resources in all formats and provides assistance for Internet usage and computer programmes within the Library.
- Provides Reader Advisory and basic instruction for all ages, as requested, for print materials, Internet usage and computer programmes.
- Sustains the dignity of patrons by giving them correct, non-judgmental and complete responses to their informational needs. Provides help where needed and respects patron's right to browse.
- Interprets and applies typical library search strategies.
- Informally assesses the community regularly to identify community needs and preferences.
- Composes bibliographies, book reviews and press releases as requested.
- Consults with peers on library matters, this may include staff meetings, workshops, Wired Montana listserve, other library listserves, professional gatherings and other resources.
- Keeps current on new library materials and technologies.
- Prepares correspondence/documentation on procedural or informational matters as needed or requested.

- Keeps Director informed as to project progression, needs and outcomes.
- Collects data and compiles reports as requested.
- Maintains and manages technological equipment (photocopier, printers, AV equipment, computers and reader/printer) requiring minimal servicing and accountability within the library, may train other staff on the use of this equipment as requested.
- Handles monetary payments for fines, donations, ILL, etc.
- Enforces library rules for the protection of library patrons and property.
- Helps to maintain a neat, clean, functional and inviting library. Provides a welcoming and safe atmosphere.
- Participates in circulation tasks, which may include checkouts, record keeping, opening and closing routines, reserves, sorting mail and other tasks associated with circulating materials.
- Plans, implements and follows through with procedural and informational duties and assists with library promotion and services as assigned.
- Assists the public, on the phone or in person, on the use, availability and status of library materials.
- Interacts with customers and staff in a courteous and professional manner and attempts to defuse and/or resolve potentially volatile or sensitive situations to ensure quality customer service.
- Recommends books and other materials to be purchased for the collection.
- Performs supervisory and professional duties requiring adherence to standards of accuracy, timeliness, tact and confidentiality.
- Participates in continuing education programmes related to library services and pursues Montana Library Certification.

Specific Priorities May Include:

Collection Development Responsibilities:

- Researches, evaluates and oversees all adult acquisitions by reviewing, selecting, weeding and maintaining the materials.
- Coordinates staff and patron recommendations and suggestions for adult library materials and considers the opinions and requests of patrons in the development and evaluation of the adult library services.
- Orders all of the adult acquisitions through jobbers, suppliers and other sources.
- Consults with technical services for assessing the best possible access to the collection by users.
- Supervises and manages the magazine and newspaper collection. This includes recording, labelling, distributing and weeding.
- Appraises and evaluates gift items to maximize the benefit to the library's collection.

Reference Responsibilities:

- Performs professional support service for patrons by undertaking difficult and complex informational and reference searches.
- Assists the public in the use of the library, providing information services via the reference interview in person or by phone; locates materials through the use of catalogues, the collection, indexes, interlibrary loan, electronic database searching and/or referral to other agencies for reference information.
- Recommends reference material acquisitions.

Community Outreach Responsibilities:

- Designs, develops, implements and budgets Community Outreach programmes for the Library.
- Promotes the Library through all media sources regularly.
- Coordinates the Community Outreach programme with agencies being served.

- Actively participates in pursuing alternative funding sources to help fund the Community Outreach programme.
- Supervises the purchasing of appropriate materials for meeting the needs of Community Outreach programmes.
- Consults and collaborates with peers in order to plan and develop community outreach programmes appropriate for the Library.
- Collects and compiles statistical data and pertinent reports about the Community Outreach programmes.
- Collaborates with Director about the direction and scope of the Community Outreach programme and keeps the Director informed about the programmes.

Other Assigned Duties May Include:

- Serving as backup person for other areas in the Library as needed.
- Other duties may be assigned.

Supervision: Under general supervision of the Library Director.

Responsibility for Work of Others: May supervise Library Staff when they are assisting with the essential duties of the Public Services Librarian. May supervise volunteers or community workers as appropriate.

Knowledge, Skills and Abilities: Bachelor's Degree is required; course work in library science is preferred. 4 years of progressive responsibility experience in a library environment is required. Must have skills in operating personal computers including automated information database, database creation, word processing, spreadsheets and electronic software. A working knowledge of library standards and rules such as USMARC and AACR2 is essential.

Must be familiar with library tools for evaluating, acquiring and maintaining library collections. A working knowledge of office procedures is desirable. Must be able to work easily with older adult populations. Must be a capable public speaker. Must know how to use Online Public Access Catalogue, electronic resources and other information technology sources to meet typical library needs. Must be able to demonstrate the ability to use 20 reference sources, to conduct a reference interview and be able to answer reference questions with authority and thoroughness to meet patron needs. Must also know interlibrary loan processes and philosophy; OCLC protocol knowledge is desirable.

The position requires a commitment to service excellence; the ability to see the big picture of the Library; the ability to work well with others in a team; the ability to provide leadership and plan, prioritize and focus on what is critical; commitment to lifelong learning; recognition of the value of professional networking; and the ability to remain flexible and positive in a time of continuing change.

Working Conditions and Physical Demands: Physical requirements include ability to move around the facility, walk, sit, bend, climb, kneel, carry and stoop; Ability to use hand and finger motion with enough manual dexterity to use computers and handle library items; Lift up to 25#, or greater with assistance; and perform other efforts as identified with normal library work; must have the ability to communicate with patrons effectively; having the ability to talk with clarity and be able to listen to patrons accurately; Must have specific vision abilities (adjusted) that include close and distance vision with good depth perception; reasonable accommodations may be available; Typing ability and computer skills are essential.

Duties are performed in surroundings where undesirable physical conditions and hazards are minor and controllable

Sample 8

Job Title: Library Assistant III—Public Services. (Reference, Circulation, Special Collections and Interlibrary Loan)

Current Employee: Nancy Watts

Supervision: Under the general supervision of the Library Director

Min/Max Base Salary: ______________ FTE:______1_____

Anniversary Date:__________________ Employee Signature:

____

Position Overview: A Library Assistant III - Public Services performs professional library functions requiring specialized knowledge and expertise in all areas of public library services. This position focuses on reference, circulation, special collections and Interlibrary Loan duties. The Library Assistant III acknowledges and accepts the Library's Code of Service, respects the Library's confidentiality laws and maintains the integrity of the Lewistown Public Library.

Principle Job Duties (not all inclusive):

Principle Priorities: Duties may be assigned or modified by Director.

General:

- Aspires to help patrons to become lifelong library users by introducing them to the wealth of library resources and enables them to use library services effectively.
- Assists patrons in locating needed resources in all formats and provides assistance for Internet usage and computer programmes within the Library.
- Provides Reader Advisory and basic instruction for all ages, as requested, for print materials, Internet usage and computer programmes.
- Sustains the dignity of patrons by giving them correct, non-judgmental and complete responses to their informational needs. Provides help where needed and respects patron's right to browse.
- Interprets and applies typical library search strategies.
- Informally assesses the community regularly to identify community needs and preferences.
- Composes bibliographies, book reviews and press releases as requested.
- Consults with peers on library matters, this may include staff meetings, workshops, Wired Montana listserve, other library listserves, professional gatherings and other resources.
- Keeps current on new library materials and technologies.
- Prepares correspondence/documentation on procedural or informational matters as needed or requested.

- Keeps Director informed as to project progression, needs and outcomes.
- Collects data and compiles reports as requested.
- Maintains and manages technological equipment (photocopier, printers, AV equipment, computers and reader/printer) requiring minimal servicing and accountability within the library, may train other staff on the use of this equipment as requested.
- Handles monetary payments for fines, donations, ILL, etc.
- Enforces library rules for the protection of library patrons and property.
- Helps to maintain a neat, clean, functional and inviting library. Provides a welcoming and safe atmosphere.
- Participates in circulation tasks, which may include checkouts, record keeping, opening and closing routines, reserves, sorting mail and other tasks associated with circulating materials.
- Plans, implements and follows through with procedural and informational duties and assists with library promotion and services as assigned.
- Assists the public, on the phone or in person, on the use, availability and status of library materials.
- Interacts with customers and staff in a courteous and professional manner and attempts to defuse and/or resolve potentially volatile or sensitive situations to ensure quality customer service.
- Recommends books and other materials to be purchased for the collection.
- Performs supervisory and professional duties requiring adherence to standards of accuracy, timeliness, tact and confidentiality.
- Participates in continuing education programmes related to library services and pursues Montana Library Certification.

Specific:

Reference Responsibilities:

- Performs professional support service in a designated collection of materials requiring specialized knowledge and demonstrated expertise in one or more functional areas of the library: reference, adult non-fiction, Montana Collection, Photograph Archives and other Special Collections.
- Assesses, inventories and weeds the adult reference and non-fiction collections. Makes recommendations for status of library materials, changes and imports/exports MARC records as appropriate.
- Performs difficult and complex informational and reference service.
- Maintains a system of inter-related files and records.
- Trains and supervises staff in use and uniqueness of the reference collection.
- Assists the public in the use of the library, providing information services via the reference interview in person or by phone; locates materials through catalogues, shelves, indexes, interlibrary loan, electronic database searching and/or referral to other agencies for reference information.
- Recommends reference and non-fiction material acquisitions.

Special Collections Responsibilities:

- Assesses, inventories and indexes the Montana Collection, other Special Collections and the Photograph Archives. Appraises and acquires local history information to be added to the collection.
- Coordinates with other agencies (public or private) and local history groups to promote the area's history.
- Develops programmes and displays pertaining to the Montana Collection, the Special Collection and the Photograph Archives.
- Trains and supervises staff in the Special collections uniqueness.

Circulation Responsibilities:

- Configures the circulation database, establishing and maintaining the accuracy of circulation privileges, patron maintenance and parameters including loan options, renewal and fine calculations, reserves, notices or messages.
- Supervises and directs circulation and has responsibility for its daily operation.
- Supervises and trains staff and volunteers in circulation procedures.
- Performs circulation duties including: checking books in and out, collecting fines, recording daily statistics, processing reserves, tracking the meeting room schedule, registering new borrowers. It also includes generating daily, monthly and annual statistics reports, mailing overdue notices, recording delinquent items and overseeing the back up of the automated system.
- Recommends operating policies, procedures and practices or methods for circulation. Implements changes upon the approval of the Director.
- Prepares daily cash balances, makes periodic deposits to the city office and maintains the cash register.

Interlibrary Loan (ILL) Responsibilities:

- Responsible for organizing the Interlibrary Loan procedures through Passport and OCLC/LaserCat. This includes borrowing materials, returning materials and recommending policies and procedures for Interlibrary Loan.
- Reviews and updates the status of requests and monitors the timely return of materials.
- Responds to any queries from patrons and other libraries regarding loaned materials and sends notices to library users of overdue material.
- Assists staff and patrons with Interlibrary Loan procedures, including Passport, OCLC/LaserCat.
- Keeps accurate records of transactions and data, including

monthly and annual statistics of all Interlibrary Loan processes.

- Completes a yearly report for Interlibrary Loan reimbursement from Montana State Library.
- Orders and inventories postage for Interlibrary Loan and the Library. Prepares packages for mailing items.
- Stays current with Interlibrary Loan procedures and policies with OCLC/WLN and the Montana State Library's rules and regulations through continuing education.

Other Assigned Duties may include:

- Serving as the backup person for technical services and other library areas as needed.
- Ordering, filing and inventorying the Income Tax display.
- Other duties may be assigned.

Supervision: Under general supervision of the Library Director.

Responsibility for Work of Others: May supervise Library Staff when they are assisting with the essential duties of the Public Services Librarian. May supervise volunteers or community workers as appropriate.

Knowledge, Skills and Abilities: Bachelor's Degree required; course work in library science is preferred. 4 years progressive responsibility experience in a library environment is required. Must have skills in operating personal computers including automated information database, database creation, word processing, spreadsheets and electronic software. A working knowledge of library standards and rules such as USMARC and AACR2 is essential.

Must be familiar with library tools for evaluating, acquiring and maintaining library collections. A working knowledge of office procedures is desirable. Must know how to use Online Public Access Catalogue, electronic resources and other information technology sources to meet typical library needs. Must be familiar with library tools for evaluating, acquiring and maintaining library collections. Must be able to demonstrate the ability to use 20 reference sources, to conduct a reference interview and be able to answer reference questions with authority and thoroughness to meet patron needs. Must also know interlibrary loan processes and philosophy; OCLC protocol knowledge is essential.

The position requires a commitment to service excellence; the ability to see the big picture of the Library; the ability to work well with others in a team; the ability to provide leadership and plan, prioritize and focus on what is critical; commitment to lifelong learning; recognition of the value of professional networking; and the ability to remain flexible and positive in a time of continuing change.

Working Conditions and Physical Demands: Physical requirements include ability to move around the facility, walk, sit, bend, climb, kneel, carry and stoop; Ability to use hand and finger motion with enough manual dexterity to use computers and handle library items; Lift up to 25#, or greater with assistance; and perform other efforts as identified with normal library work; must have the ability to communicate with patrons effectively; having the ability to talk with clarity and be able to listen to patrons accurately; Must have specific vision abilities (adjusted) that include close and distance vision with good depth perception; reasonable accommodations may be available; Typing ability and computer skills are essential.

Duties are performed in surroundings where undesirable physical conditions and hazards are minor and controllable.

Sample 9

Job Title: Library Assistant III - Technical Services (Information Management and Technical Processing)

Current Employee:

Supervision: Under the general supervision of the Library Director

Min/Max Base Salary: ____________ FTE:__________

Anniversary Date:______________. Employee Signature:

____

Position Overview: A Library Assistant III - Technical Services performs professional library functions requiring specialized knowledge and expertise in all areas of public library services. This position focuses on the technical processing of all library materials and information management of library technology. The Library Assistant III acknowledges and accepts the Library's Code of Service, respects the Library's confidentiality laws and the integrity of the Lewistown Public Library.

Principle Priorities: Duties may be assigned or modified by Director.

General:

- Aspires to help patrons to become lifelong library users by introducing them to the wealth of library resources and enables them to use library services effectively.
- Assists patrons in locating needed resources in all formats and provides assistance for Internet usage and computer programmes within the Library.
- Provides Reader Advisory and basic instruction for all ages, as requested, for print materials, Internet usage and computer programmes.
- Sustains the dignity of patrons by giving them correct, non-judgmental and complete responses to their informational needs. Provides help where needed and respects patron's right to browse.
- Interprets and applies typical library search strategies.
- Informally assesses the community regularly to identify community needs and preferences.
- Composes bibliographies, book reviews and press releases as requested.
- Consults with peers on library matters, this may include staff meetings, workshops, Wired Montana listserve, other library listserves, professional gatherings and other resources.
- Keeps current on new library materials and technologies.
- Prepares correspondence/documentation on procedural or informational matters as needed or requested.
- Keeps Director informed as to project progression, needs and outcomes.

- Collects data and compiles reports as requested.
- Maintains and manages technological equipment (photocopier, printers, AV equipment, computers and reader/printer) requiring minimal servicing and accountability within the library, may train other staff on the use of this equipment as requested.
- Handles monetary payments for fines, donations, ILL, etc.
- Enforces library rules for the protection of library patrons and property.
- Helps to maintain a neat, clean, functional and inviting library. Provides a welcoming and safe atmosphere.
- Participates in circulation tasks, which may include checkouts, record keeping, opening and closing routines, reserves, sorting mail and other tasks associated with circulating materials.
- Plans, implements and follows through with procedural and informational duties and assists with library promotion and services as assigned.
- Assists the public, on the phone or in person, on the use, availability and status of library materials.
- Interacts with customers and staff in a courteous and professional manner and attempts to defuse and/or resolve potentially volatile or sensitive situations to ensure quality customer service.
- Recommends books and other materials to be purchased for the collection.
- Performs supervisory and professional duties requiring adherence to standards of accuracy, timeliness, tact and confidentiality.
- Participates in continuing education programmes related to library services and pursues Montana Library Certification.

Specific Priorities:

Information Management Responsibilities:

- Develops, directs and implements the criteria for the acquisition of all MARC21 record information for the

Library's collection following Montana State Library, AACR2 and Library of Congress rules and regulations.

- Assists in the assessment, evaluation, configuring and monitoring of library technology and other resources for automated library services including the appropriate technology products used in the Library (*e.g.*, Follett applications, LaserCat, Internet, CatExpress, Passport, UltraCard MARC, CD-ROMs, electronic databases, etc.).
- Supervises, configures and implements the library database programmes such as Circulation Plus, Cataloging Plus, OPAC, Follett Applications, Passport, CatExpress, Ultra Card MARC and LaserCat databases, establishing and maintaining their accuracy.
- Assists and coordinates with school and public librarians on library technology and cataloging aspects. Maintains and expands knowledge of library technology and services.
- Assists in the development of policies and procedures for delivering technical services and information to users and staff.

Technical Processing Responsibilities:

- Maintains specialized reports, statistical and data analyses and other information to provide accurate and concise feedback about the Lewistown Public Library for various entities.
- Assists and trains staff in areas of technical data interpretation and manipulations for the Library's system.
- Assists in the determination of placement, genre and classifications of library materials within the collection.
- Catalogues all Library materials in full MARC21 format with accuracy and adherence to established library standards such as AACR2 and Library of Congress using both copycat and original cataloging methods.
- Manages all original and copycat bibliographic records that are added to and/or corrected in the Library's local automated system. Massages data as needed to be interpreted and useful in the Library's automated system using cataloging methods such as: Online Passport or

TTY, Batch-load/tape-loading systems, CatExpress Web and bibliographic utilities like OCLC and WLN/OCLC LaserCat, etc.

- Oversees the exporting/importing of electronic bibliographic MARC records and holdings data in batch/single file format from online sessions of OCLC WorldCat, CatExpress and/or Passport, etc. to/from the Library's automated catalogue system and sends updates to WLN/OCLC quarterly with holdings data.
- Oversees all aspects of the physical processing of library materials including supervising of assistants.
- Assesses, inventories, discards and processes collections with collaboration with other staff.

Other Assigned Duties May Include:

- Serving as a backup person for other library areas as needed.
- Other duties as assigned.

Supervision: Under general supervision of the Library Director.

Responsibility for Work of Others: May supervise Library Staff when they are assisting with the essential duties of the Technical Services area. May supervise volunteers or community workers as appropriate.

Knowledge, Skills and Abilities: Bachelor's Degree is required; course work in library science is preferred. 4 years of progressive responsibility experience in a library environment is required or a lesser experience in an actual cataloging position dealing with electronic information data, assessment and cataloging skills would be considered. Must have skills in operating personal computers including automated information database, database creation, word processing, spreadsheets and electronic software. A thorough knowledge of library standards and rules such as USMARC and AACR2 is essential. Must be familiar with library tools for evaluating, acquiring and maintaining library collections. Must know how to use an Online Public Access Catalogue and other information technology sources to meet typical library needs.

Must also know interlibrary loan process and philosophy; OCLC protocol knowledge is desirable. Must have a thorough knowledge of the concepts and theories of library science and cataloging, experience with specialized technology related to library information retrieval, management and services delivery. A working knowledge of typical office procedures is desirable. Must be able to demonstrate the ability to conduct a reference interview and be able to answer reference questions with authority and thoroughness to meet patron needs.

The position requires a commitment to service excellence; the ability to see the big picture of the Library; the ability to work well with others in a team; the ability to provide leadership and plan, prioritize and focus on what is critical; commitment to lifelong learning; recognition of the value of professional networking; and the ability to remain flexible and positive in a time of continuing change.

Working Conditions and Physical Demands: Physical requirements include ability to move around the facility, walk, sit, bend, carry and stoop; Ability to use hand and finger motion with enough manual dexterity to use computers and handle library items; Typing ability and computer skills are essential. A minimum typing speed of 50 WPM with a 95% accuracy rate is essential. Lift up to 25#, or greater with assistance; and perform other efforts as identified with normal library work; must have the ability to communicate with patrons effectively; having the ability to talk with clarity and be able to listen to patrons accurately; Must have specific vision abilities (adjusted) that include close and distance vision with good depth perception; reasonable accommodations may be available.

Duties are performed in surroundings where undesirable physical conditions and hazards are minor and controllable.

Part-time Employee

Sample 1

Job Description: Part-Time Person

Daily: Circulation procedures including:

1. Stamp enough date due cards for the day

2. Check in and shelve books
3. Straighten book shelves; (edge, leave 6 inches space at end of shelf if possible) make sure spine labels are attached; "wash" dirty books; make sure picture books, easy readers, board books and juvenile fiction are correctly shelved.
4. Keep children's area neat and inviting.
5. Call people whose books are on reserve shelf. Flag titles that people reserve.
6. Shelve Locked Case materials.
7. Straighten reference collection. Report any mission volumes to librarian.
8. Other duties as assigned.

Weekly:

1. Put picture books, easy readers, juvenile fiction in order.
2. Replace books sold from the book sale cart with sale books from downstairs.
3. Other duties as assigned.

Monthly:

1. Record circulation statistics.
2. Box and label McNaughton books which librarian has pulled from collection.
3. Type board meeting minutes.
4. Other duties as assigned.

Yearly:

1. Assist librarian with annual report.
2. Other duties as assigned.

Ongoing:

1. Assist with cataloging as needed.
2. Work on annual inventory.
3. Assist with book orders.
4. Delete books as requested by librarian.
5. Other duties as assigned.

Major Project:

1. Plan, organize and implement story times.
2. Familiarize yourself with the children's "stuff" in office, with bottom file cabinet outside the office and in basement.
3. Work with Laurie to clean the poster and craft mess downstairs.

Professional Librarian

Sample 1

Nature of Work: Positions in this class perform responsible professional, supervisory and administrative library work.

The tasks performed involve functioning independently as the supervisor of at least one of the major units of the library system. Work is performed under the general administrative direction of the library director and is reviewed through conferences, reports and the efficiency of services provided.

Supevision may be exercised over paraprofessional, student, volunteer and other professional personnel.

Employees in this classification have considerable contact in writing, in person, or by telephone with patrons, co-workers, community groups and leaders and professionals in other library systems.

Work is performed at the headquarters library location and occasionally at branches and other sites, as needed.

Representative Examples of Work: Only major tasks are identified for most positions; refer to position description for detailed listing of duties.

Directs and coordinates the activities of at least one of the major functional units of the library; supervises, trains and evaluates the work of staff; communicates library policy to subordinates and the public.

Participates in library planning by meeting with the library director and other library unit heads; coordinates with the various units of the library in daily operations and in long range planning for the full library programme; contributes to preparation of the annual library budget in area of responsibility.

Assumes responsibility for the library, as delegated, in the absence of the director; responds to security problems in the area of responsibility and overall responsibility for building, security, as needed.

Participates in materials selection; plans and implements portions of library public relations efforts; initiates and evaluates programmes. Performs related work as assigned.

Selection Factorsl: These factors will be the basis for selecting the most qualified applicants to be interviewed. Applicants selected for employment must satisfactorily demonstrate possession of these factors during and after a prescribed probationary period for continued employment.

Knowledge of:

- o current library principles, methods and practices, including library administration.
- o library reference materials, equipment and procedures.
- o reader interest levels, books, authors and selection criteria.
- o cataloging and classification plans.
- o automated library procedures and applications.

Skill in:

- o operation of office equipment and modern library equipment including computer terminals.

Ability to:

- o learn and abide by Flathead County Library System policies and procedures.
- o plan and direct a major unit of a county library system.
- o plan and supervise the work of a group of professional, paraprofessional and clerical employees.
- o coordinate the activities of a major unit with other library units.
- o establish and maintain effective working, relationships with supervisor, co-workers, library patrons, other agencies and other employees.
- o correctly lift and carry up to fifty pounds.
- o work under pressure effectively.

General Recruitmfnt Indicators: Person applying for a position in this class should have the following experience and/ or training.

Graduation from an approved college or university with a master's degree in library science, media or another related degree and three years of experience in professional library work; or any equivalent combination of experience and training which indicates possession of the knowledge, skills and abilities listed.

Reference Librarian

Sample 1

Position: Reference Librarian

Department: County Library

Accountable To: Library Director

Summary of Work: Maintains and delivers library services for the community by answering requests for information and recreational reading. Uses the County Library, other libraries and other agencies to answer requests. Assists with developing the collection for public use.

Job Characteristics

Nature of Work: This position performs administrative, supervisory and professional duties requiring adherence to standards of accuracy, timeliness, tact and confidentiality. Position requires ability to move and shelve heavy books. Position works varying work schedule and includes some evenings and weekends.

Consequence of errors may result in dissatisfied library users and loss of time to find and correct mistakes.

Personal Contacts: Continual and demanding contact with the public. Coordinates duties with other employees and supervisor to complete tasks.

Supervision Received: Direction from Library Director.

Essential Functions: Position requires ability to communicate orally and in writing, retrieve and return books to shelves, type, supervise, calculate, read written material, maintain files, operate a computer, operate library machines and equipment. Maintains and applies a thorough knowledge of the library automation systems.

Areas of Job Accountability and Performance: Strives to meet the objectives of the library as established by the Board.

Serves all library users by providing reference service. Works as lead worker in the reference department and provides direction to other employees, volunteers and student workers. Makes decisions on how to best serve each library user.

Works at the circulation desk according to assigned schedule and will answer the telephone as needed.

Performs daily activities - retrieves reports, checks library materials in and out, shelves books, files, operates online catalogue and automation system. May be responsible for displays and bulletin boards within the library.

Assists with original cataloging if material is not found on the OCLC/WLN database. Completes the technical processing for audio and video cassettes.

Responsible for organizing the interlibrary loan procedures including borrowing materials and returning materials; gives notice to library users of overdue material; keeps accurate records and files; completes forms for Interlibrary loan reimbursement from Montana State Library.

Follows the collection management policy and leases new books according to the contract. Supports collection management by troubleshooting inventory problems, recommending purchases, processing new materials, evaluating gifts, assessing, weeding and maintaining a vertical file.

Performs other related duties as required.

Job Requirements

Knowledge: This position requires a thorough knowledge of the collection, library practices, procedures and techniques; reference information sources; OCLC/WLN and LaserCat programme.. A working knowledge of the laws, regulations and departmental policies pertaining to library services.

Demonstrates and practices the use of Internet, online catalogue, electronic databases and automation systems. Assist the library users in following an appropriate inquiry process including evaluating information.

Skills: This position requires skills in the use of computers and library equipment; skills in dealing with people.

Abilities: Position requires ability to: work well with patrons; complete tasks; pay attention to accuracy; work with interruptions; maintain confidentiality: stay abreast on new procedures affecting library and services; supervise assistants and volunteers; maintain effective working relationships with fellow employees, other agencies and the public, communicate clearly and effectively verbally and in writing.

Education and Experience: The above knowledge, skills, abilities are usually acquired through a combination of education and/or experience equivalent to:

- A Bachelor's Degree and three years of experience working in a public library is preferred.
- Current state certification is preferred.
- Strong interest in reading preferred.

Job Performance Standards: Evaluation of this position will be based primarily upon performance of the preceding requirements and duties. Examples of job performance criteria include, but are not limited to, the following:

- Performs assigned duties.
- Meets the objectives of the library as established by the Board.
- Effectively researches information for patrons using and evaluating electronic resources and/or other library materials and books.
- Competently processes, classifies and processes books and other library materials.
- Effectively assists all library users in the use of the library.
- Maintains confidentiality of sensitive information.
- Maintains accurate and timely records.

- Deals tactfully and courteously with the public.
- Keeps work areas neat.
- Observes work hours.
- Demonstrates punctuality.
- Establishes and maintains effective working relationships with fellow employees, supervisors and the public

Substitute Librarian

Sample 1

Position: Substitute Librarian

Accountable to: Head Librarian or Library Staff who is in charge

Summary of Work: The library sub will perform the everyday duties of the normal staff members.

Job Characteristics

- Work with the public and other staff members
- Perform the list of duties for all staff members to perform daily
- Dress in a professional manner
- Keep busy doing jobs from the list of everyday duties
- Follow the regular policies and procedures of the library
- Be extremely careful in check out and check in of books, make sure to check book pockets and cards when shelving and make sure there are no date due cards in books instead of book cards.

Job Accountability:

- Performs daily duties of the library
- Assists patrons in the use if the library, including equipment
- Performs circulation tasks efficiently
- Uses patron-free time to the best of ability (shelving, straightening shelves etc.)
- Dresses professionally
- Uses good communications skills, both written and oral

Job Requirements

Knowledge: A working knowledge of library principles, organization, operation and procedures.

Skills and Abilities: Circulation of books, library equipment, communication skills, work well with others, work on your own and carry on tasks without being told.

Education and Experience: The above skills and abilities are typically acquired through a combination of education and experience equivalent to a bachelor's degree in teaching or library science and some experience in teaching or library operations.

Job Performance Standards: Evaluation of this position will be based primarily upon the preceding job description requirements and duties. See sample list of duties above.

Youth Services Librarian

Sample 1

Job Title: Youth Services Librarian

(Youth Collection Development & Management, Youth Outreach, Youth Related Reference)

Current Employee:

Supervision: Under the general supervision of the Library Director

Min/Max Base Salary: ______________ FTE:__________

Anniversary Date:________________ Employee Signature:

____

Position Overview: A Youth Services Librarian performs professional library functions requiring specialized knowledge and expertise in all areas of public library services especially those areas relating to toddler, school aged children and young adults; parents, caregivers and educators. This position focuses on management of the Youth Services department, development and management of the youth collection, youth related community outreach and youth related reference responsibilities. The Youth Services Librarian acknowledges and accepts the Library's Code of Service, respects the Library's confidentiality laws and maintains the integrity of the Lewistown Public Library.

Principle Priorities: Duties may be assigned or modified by Director.

General:

- Aspires to help patrons to become lifelong library users by introducing them to the wealth of library resources and enables them to use library services effectively.
- Assists patrons in locating needed resources in all formats and provides assistance for Internet usage and computer programmes within the Library.
- Provides Reader Advisory and basic instruction for all ages, as requested, for print materials, Internet usage and computer programmes.
- Sustains the dignity of patrons by giving them correct, non-judgmental and complete responses to their informational needs. Provides help where needed and respects patron's right to browse.
- Interprets and applies typical library search strategies.
- Informally assesses the community regularly to identify community needs and preferences.
- Composes bibliographies, book reviews and press releases as requested.
- Consults with peers on library matters, this may include staff meetings, workshops, Wired Montana listserve, other library listserves, professional gatherings and other resources.
- Keeps current on new library materials and technologies.
- Prepares correspondence/documentation on procedural or informational matters as needed or requested.
- Keeps Director informed as to project progression, needs and outcomes.
- Collects data and compiles reports as requested.
- Maintains and manages technological equipment (photocopier, printers, AV equipment, computers and reader/printer) requiring minimal servicing and

accountability within the library, may train other staff on the use of this equipment as requested.

- Handles monetary payments for fines, donations, ILL, etc.
- Enforces library rules for the protection of library patrons and property.
- Helps to maintain a neat, clean, functional and inviting library. Provides a welcoming and safe atmosphere.
- Participates in circulation tasks, which may include checkouts, record keeping, opening and closing routines, reserves, sorting mail and other tasks associated with circulating materials.
- Plans, implements and follows through with procedural and informational duties and assists with library promotion and services as assigned.
- Assists the public, on the phone or in person, on the use, availability and status of library materials.
- Interacts with customers and staff in a courteous and professional manner and attempts to defuse and/or resolve potentially volatile or sensitive situations to ensure quality customer service.
- Recommends books and other materials to be purchased for the collection.
- Performs supervisory and professional duties requiring adherence to standards of accuracy, timeliness, tact and confidentiality.
- Participates in continuing education programmes related to library services and pursues Montana Library Certification.

Specific Priorities:

Youth Services Area Responsibilities:

- Responsible for the Youth Services Department. Plans, organizes and implements services and materials for youth, ages pre-school through high school, educators, parents and teachers, to instill a life long love of reading and learning.

- Maintains direct contact with community resource people so that children and adults working with children can be referred to appropriate sources of assistance. Knowledge of the community and client group is obtained through regular assessment
- Provides Reader Advisory for print, Internet sites and computer programmes, specifically appropriate to reading level and interest for all ages.
- Provides educational support to school age children, (home school, public and private classrooms) and educational organizations.
- Composes bibliographies, book reviews, book-talks, library displays, press releases and other special tools to increase access to library resources, motivate their use and promote reading and library programmes.
- Provides Library tours, special story times and book talks.
- Provides instruction on library skills, research skills and usage as needed.
- Gathers materials for teachers' and classroom use as requested.
- Maintains an attractive and functional youth area.
- Provides research and assistance for homework assignments and individual pursuits, via the physical collection, Internet sources and Interlibrary Loan.
- Plans, prepares and implements regular pre-school story times that may include crafts.
- Plans, prepares and implements programmes for older youth.
- Manages the youth area computer lab, including instruction for CD Rom programmes, word processing, computer usage, Internet access and search strategies.

Youth Collection Management Responsibilities:

- Researches, evaluates and manages the youth collection by reviewing, selecting, ordering, weeding and maintaining all of the Youth Services materials. May recommend library materials for the main collection.

- Determines reading and interest levels and placement within the collection.
- Considers the opinions and requests of patrons in the development and evaluation of youth library services.
- Consults with technical services for assessing the best possible access to the collection by users.
- Consults with public services to coordinate the youth and adult areas to meet the needs of users.
- Supervises the youth magazine collection.
- Appraises and evaluates gift items to maximize the benefit to the library's youth collection.

Reference Responsibilities:

- Performs professional support service for patrons by undertaking difficult and complex informational and reference searches.
- Assists youth in the use of the library, providing information services via the reference interview in person or by phone.
- Understands and applies search strategies age appropriate to the critical thinking processes of children, to give youth access to information from the widest possible range of sources-children's and adult reference works, catalogues, indexes, electronic database searching, interlibrary loan, information and referral files and /or referral to other agencies for reference information.
- Manages the youth reference acquisitions with assessment, selection, evaluation, ordering and weeding of the materials.
- Provides readers advisory service in reference.
- Prepares correspondence on procedural or informational matters especially related to the youth area and keeps the Director informed.

Community Outreach Responsibilities:

- Provides offsite school programmes, such as storytelling and book talks, assemblies and classroom and teacher visits.

- Plans, prepares, promotes and implements a summer reading programme. Actively participates in pursuing alternative funding sources to help fund the youth outreach programmes and purchases materials needed.
- Designs, develops, implements and budgets other youth outreach programmes for the Library.
- Promotes the Library through media sources regularly.
- Coordinates youth outreach programmes with agencies being served.
- Consults and collaborates with peers in order to plan and develop youth outreach programmes appropriate for the Library.
- Collects and compiles statistical data and pertinent reports about the youth outreach programmes.
- Collaborates with Director about the direction and scope of the youth outreach programme and keeps the Director informed about the programmes.

Other Assigned Duties May Include:

- Serving as backup person for director and other library areas as needed.
- Other duties may be assigned.

Supervision: Under general supervision of the Library Director.

Responsibility for Work of Others: May supervise Library Staff when they are assisting with the essential duties in the Youth Services Area. May supervise volunteers or community workers as appropriate.

Knowledge, Skills and Abilities: Masters in Library or Information Science degree with emphasis upon youth services is preferred; Required: a Bachelor's Degree with some course work in library science; 5 years experience in a library environment. Essential Skills/Abilities: demonstrates knowledge of child development and the reading acquisition process; knowledge and appreciation of children's and young adult literature, audiovisual materials, computer resources and other materials that constitute a balanced, relevant youth collection; knowledge of reference materials and other library resources which may serve the needs of children and their care givers; demonstrates good interpersonal skills in meeting with children, parents, staff and community; demonstrates good active listening skills. Must be an effective and capable public speaker. Must be able to conduct multiple age story times or programmes with sensitivity to the various needs of the audience and with age appropriate materials and activities.

A working knowledge of library standards and rules such as USMARC and AACR2 is essential. Must be familiar with library tools for evaluating, acquiring and maintaining library collections. Must know how to use Online Public Access Catalogue, electronic resources and other information technology sources to meet typical library needs. Must demonstrate the ability to conduct a reference interview and be able to answer reference questions with authority and tenacity to meet patron needs. Must have skills in operating personal computers, automated information databases, database creation, word processing, spreadsheets and electronic software. A working knowledge of office procedures is desirable.

The position requires a commitment to service excellence; the ability to see the big picture of the Library; the ability to work well with others in a team; the ability to provide leadership and plan, prioritize and focus on what is critical; commitment to lifelong learning; recognition of the value of professional networking; and the ability to remain flexible and positive in a time of continuing change.

Working Conditions and Physical Demands: Physical requirements include ability to move around the facility, walk, sit, bend, climb, kneel, carry and stoop; Ability to use hand and finger motion with enough manual dexterity to use computers and handle library items; Lift up to 25#, or greater with assistance; and perform other efforts as identified with normal library work; must have the ability to communicate with patrons effectively; having the ability to talk with clarity and be able to listen to patrons accurately; Must have specific vision abilities (adjusted) that include close and distance vision with good depth perception; reasonable accommodations may be available;

Typing ability and computer skills are essential. Duties are performed in surroundings where undesirable physical conditions and hazards are minor and controllable.

Improving their Accuracy and Usefulness

The first stage of the research project consisted of a literature review. The review was limited to literature published between 1988 and 1998 as I was interested in examining job descriptions in today's work context rather than from a historical perspective.

LaRoory (1995) describes three main attitudes towards job descriptions. These are:

- the campaigners who believe up to date job descriptions are essential for the effective running of any organisation;
- the neutrals who are probably the largest group and are neither for nor against job descriptions. This group usually does not use job descriptions for managing their area of responsibility; and
- the contras who believe job descriptions are not necessary or desirable. They think that anything written down about a job is likely to be out of date by the next month, if not sooner.

This appears to be an accurate representation as I experienced all three attitudes when discussing job descriptions with staff from various organisations during the research project. People were either very enthusiastic, couldn't care less - 'yes we do have them but they are not used much' - or felt they were a waste of time, energy and money.

What is a Job Rescription?

Sahl, (1994. p.3) states 'well written job descriptions define the work of the organisation and its reasons for existence as an employer of human resources. More, they define and help quantify the relative importance of work, what each position contributes to a process and the organisation as a whole.' This definition illustrates an important point regarding job descriptions, used in today's work environment, by emphasising that they describe not only what the job is about but how the job contributes to the work of the organisation.

A job description must be accurate but not a minutely detailed list of an employees tasks and duties (DeLon, 1994). As Behn (1997, p. 60) states: 'it is impossible to list, in anything smaller than an encyclopedia, the multitude of tasks ... that combine to produce the results desired from a particular job.' Job descriptions are meant to be a guide only 'staff must not interpret them rigidly or job descriptions become a barrier to success' (Degner, 1995, p. 17). Grant (1989) describes them as a 'map' that show direction. Job descriptions are not a description of how a job is to be done (Grant, 1989), a contract (DeLon, 1994) or set of rules, regulations or proper practices (Grant, 1989). They describe the nature of the work to be done by stating the purpose and main responsibilities. They may also include information on the type of person who is best suited to perform the job.

Grant (1988) describes job descriptions as a valuable resource. They have the potential to be a useful organisational tool, however, to realise their potential they must be properly prepared. Grant (1988, p. 53) believes many job descriptions do not reach their potential because they 'are too simplistic, they lack detail, they are out of date, they neglect many key structural elements of the job and they are unclearly written'.

There are two main types of job descriptions, the generic or general and the specific or individual. Generic job descriptions are written in broadly stated general terms without identifying specific responsibilities, requirements, purpose and relationships. Some organisations use generic job descriptions for the same level within an organisation. For particular positions an additional duty statement may be developed. Specific job descriptions provide information on all essential responsibilities assigned to the person performing the job, they are usually quite detailed and comprehensive. (How to write job descriptions the easy way, 1993)

Why are Job Descriptions Important?

Ray and Hawthorne (1993, p i) state 'an accurate and detailed job description is an increasingly crucial component of the effective use of valuable human resources in libraries and other organisations.' The primary function of a job description is as a communication tool. They effectively communicate a great deal of information about a job, especially between the manager and employee (Giles, 1995; Grant, 1989). 'When employees have a road map to success they often perform much better - and that translates into continued business growth for you and your firm' (Consulting Task Force, 1991). Information may include reporting relationships; skill requirements; major responsibilities; where the job fits into the organisation and what is required of the position. This information is presented in a completely objective and impersonal way (How to write job descriptions the easy way, 1993) which allows the job description to be used in relation to many human resource functions such as recruitment, induction, training and performance management.

Well written job descriptions also provide information to prospective employees about organisational expectations of a particular job (Carlopio, 1996). This aids in retaining staff as the more a prospective employee knows about the culture of an organisation and what is expected of them, the quicker they will settle into the organisation. Unclear job descriptions, which do not describe organisational information and expectations, may mislead a new employee. 'A major barrier to the formation of organisational commitment is a large gap between what people expect and what the realities turn out to be' (Carlopio, 1986, p.58).

What are Job Descriptions Used for?

Job descriptions have the potential to be used for a number of human resource functions. The main purposes reported in the literature include the following. Again the emphasis is on well written job descriptions.

- Selection and recruitment. Job descriptions may be used to advertise jobs, screen applicants, develop questions for the job interview and identify essential and desirable criteria.
- Induction and orientation. Job descriptions provide a good introduction and overview of the job which enables the employee to understand what the organisation expects of them.

- Understanding the employee's role in the organisation. Job descriptions allow the employee to see where they fit into the big picture of the organisation and how their job contributes to the organisation. They may also reflect organisational goals and objectives.
- Identifying training requirements. Job descriptions may identify initial training requirements for a new employee. If they are included in a performance management system they may be used as an aid in identifing training to improve performance or additional training needed as a result of changing responsibilities.
- Performance management. Job descriptions are the foundation of an effective performance management system (Meng, 1992) and are used in conducting performance reviews or job evaluations. They may also be used to develop performance measures (Russell, 1996). However, it is important to note that job descriptions are only one component of an effective performance management system. Such a system includes other processes and documentation. For example, an organisation may have induction policies and programme, identified roles and responsibilities of various levels of staff, a rewards and recognition programme and performance appraisal system.
- Career development. A study of job descriptions can help employees determine what qualifications, experience and skills are needed to apply for different positions within the organisation. This information can then be used in career planning or development.

Other purposes listed in the literature include:

- orienting new supervisors on what their subordinates and bosses do (Grant 1989)
- analysing work flows and methods (Plachy and Plachy, 1993)
- mentoring (DeLon, 1994)
- industrial relations (Drummond, 1994)
- job restructuring (Drummond, 1994)

- determining what kinds of assignments are given to employees (Bust 1990, Lemos, 1994)
- organisational and personal goal setting (Giles, 1995)
- conducting an organisational audit (Drummond, 1994)
- defining or reviewing organisational structure (Plachy and Plachy, 1993)
- measuring accurate salary administration (Russell, 1996)
- preparing and analysising job descriptions help assure jobs are well designed and that all sections work together to achieve the organisational aims (Grant, 1989)
- quickly preparing substitute workers or temporary help (Grant, 1989)

What is Included in a Job Description?

The content of the job description varies widely from organisation to organisation and the purpose of the job description will influence what is included. The following list outlines the most commonly referred to components of a job description (apart from the job title, identifying code, grade/ level, department, name of company, physical location, job status, date and name of incumbent) described in the literature reviewed:

- job function or purpose which explains the general purpose of the job and why it exists. It also provides the reader with a concise overview of the job.
- duties or tasks includes a precise specific list of what the employee does and is expected to do.
- responsibilities are a summary of the main responsibilities required of the position. Other terms used include Critical Success Factors (Herman and Herman, 1995) or work functions.
- accountabilities outline the major results expected from the job.
- organisational relationships outline how the job fits into the organisation and the structure of the organisation.
- working environment identifies the physical and social contexts in which the job is performed. It may also include working conditions.

- personal contacts refer to the people the employee will interact with while performing the job.
- reporting relationships include whom the employee reports to and what supervision the employee exercises.
- authority identifies what decisions the employee can make and resources they can commit.
- performance standards identify specific standards which can be used to determine whether the job is being performed satisfactorily. Other titles used include outcomes, measures of accomplishment or expected outputs.
- skills including competencies, knowledge and abilities required to perform the job.
- education or qualifications refers to qualifications needed for the job. This may also include training requirements.
- experience refers to the type and nature of experience needed to perform the job.

Other components discussed in the literature include:

- managers expectations (Osbourne, 1992)
- career mobility (DeLapa, 1989)
- position(s) previously held (DeLapa, 1989)
- meetings to attend/reports to be completed (DeLapa, 1989)
- management information required to be passed out from the job (Drummond, 1994)
- time percentages (Grant, 1996)
- scope and impact of the job (Sattler, 1993)

Format of Job Descriptions

The layout and format of the job description is very important as a clear format will aid in understanding the document. Before deciding on a format, the organisation firstly needs to consider what the job description will be used for (Grant, 1989). Once a format is decided it needs to be standardised across the organisation (Osborne, 1992; DeLon, 1994). Present tense should be used (Kramer, 1997) as the job description refers to what the person is doing, not what they have done.

The literature varies on the recommended length of job descriptions. DeLapa (1989) suggests 1-3 pages whereas Giles (1995) recommends no longer than two pages.

Different Approaches to Job Descriptions

Moravec and Tucker (1992) describes how British Petroleum replaced job descriptions with a matrix reflecting skills and behaviours. This matrix focuses on skills and behavious rather than individual jobs. Each skill matrix describes steps in the career ladder, from the lowest to the highest, along the vertical axis. The horizontal axis describes the skills and competencies that are required for each step. Moravec and Tucker (1992, p. 43) argue that 'skill matrices differ significantly from job descriptions, they specify roles and levels of performance rather than jobs in a box.' Through this system managers know what to expect of their employees and employees know what the organisation expects of them.

La Roory (1995) discusses a different approach to job descriptions by defining jobs in terms of a 'contribution matrix' (p.47). This matrix identifies team outputs and contributions made by each member within a team. Agreed outputs are written along the vertical and team members' names along the horizontal. Under each output the processes and contributions made by each team member are listed. The output is then assigned to the person who has the overall responsibility. La Roory (1995) argues that some of the advantages of this approach is that it focuses on the whole department rather than the individual job, incorporates team involvement, can be used to show use of resources and is a good vehicle to identify improvement opportunities.

Trends in the Literature

Figure identifies the main developmental trends of job descriptions identified through the literature review. While this project did not aim to identify historical trends it became clear while reviewing the literature, that even though the basic format and style of the job description has not changed greatly, the focus of the job description has changed over the last 10-15 years. Job descriptions that suited the work environment in the 1980's are referred to as traditional job descriptions. It is important to note that many authors and organisations still focus on the traditional job description format in today's work environment.

Traditional Job Descriptions vs. Job Descriptions Today

Traditional job descriptions	*Job descriptions today*
Focus on what a person is required to do - that is, a list of duties	Focus on major responsibility areas, results and outputs the person is expected to achieve
Looks at the job from an inside-out approach	Looks at the job from an outside-in approach
Written by the human resource department	Written by affected employee and manager in consultation with the human resource department
Statement included - 'and any other duties assigned by the supervisor'	The job description is seen as a profile that describes major responsibilities rather than covering everything an employee does
Access to job descriptions by affected employee and management	Job descriptions for all positions are available for any staff member to see and are used as a career development tool
Individualistic in nature - appear to focus on the job alone	Job descriptions reflect the interdependence of the job within an organisation
Reviewed when a job becomes vacant or reclassified	Incorporated into the organisation's performance management system and reviewed regularly with the employee to maintain currency, accuracy and relevance
Time, percentages or frequency included	Performance measures or indicators are included

A noticeable shift, outlined in the literature, is that job descriptions today focus on major responsibility areas rather than duties. Duties represent the methods by which the responsibility areas are accomplished. Responsibilities are like mini-jobs that must be done to get the total job successfully completed. In a fast changing work environment, responsibility areas generally remain constant whereas, duties change constantly with advances in technology and improvements to processes (Segall, 1989). Focusing on duties make it difficult to keep a job description current and does not represent the true nature of the job to be performed. When focusing on responsibilities it is important that these relate to meeting organisational objectives (DeLapa,1989).

The following quote illustrates this point:

'The duty statement is an anachronism left over from the days of rigid bureaucracies with pyramid hierarchies. But in these days of multiskilled people working in self managing teams, the traditional job description has all the value of a parachute that opens on the second bounce.' (Job descriptions? Burn the bloody things, 1995)

In addition, job descriptions have moved from focusing on what a person is required to do (that is, their duties) to focusing on the results or outputs the person is required to achieve. 'An employee can perform duties endlessly without ever accomplishing anything of value. To be truly effective job descriptions must specify what results are to be achieved.' (Plachy, 1991, p. 8) This perspective of focusing on what the person is required to do implies looking at the job from an inside out approach. However, when focusing on the end results it implies looking at the job from an outside-in approach. (Job descriptions? Burn the bloody things, 1995). Focusing on end results helps employees understand why the work is important. Knowing the results also allows employees to discover new ways to accomplish results (Plachy and Plachy, 1993) thus encouraging initiative and creativity.

In the past, the Human Resource department wrote job descriptions with little or no input from the employee actually doing the job. Today's job descriptions are usually written by the affected employee and manager (Langdon, 1996) or by the team that the job is a part of. The Human Resource department now provides a consulting role in the development of job descriptions and their job is to show managers how to define jobs (Langdon, 1996). This approach provides a more accurate job description as it is the employee and manager who have the best insight into the job and are aware of the responsibilities and results expected. Employee involvement also creates ownership (Degner, 1995).

As mentioned, job descriptions are not meant to list every duty an employee performs. However, in the past many job descriptions included statements such as 'and other duties and responsibilities that may be required on either a temporary or permanent basis' (Consulting Task Force, 1991). This allowed managers to change duties or add duties without discussing this with employees.

In today's organisation job descriptions are marketed differently in that they are promoted to staff as a job profile outlining the main responsibilities, not all the duties that need to be performed. Changes to these responsibilities are discussed between the manager and employee.

If job descriptions are to be used as a career development tool they need to be available for all staff within an organisation. Some organisations make them available online through their Intranet. This often was not the case in the past where job descriptions were only available to the person doing the job, their manager and senior management.

Traditional job descriptions were often described in a way that implied complete independence from other positions within the organisation and were very individualistic in nature. When reading this type of job descriptions it is unclear what role the job has in the organisation or how it is related to other positions and processes within the organisation.

This type of description encourages independent rather than group action (Dunn, 1993). Job descriptions today need to reflect the interdependence of processes and people within the organisation. If the organisation is based on teams and employees are expected to work together to accomplish objectives and goals, this needs to be reflected in the job description.

Job descriptions were often only reviewed when a job became vacant or new duties were added. In today's work environment job descriptions are incorporated into the organisations performance management system in order to ensure they are reviewed regularly with the employee (Carlopio, 1996). This maintains currency, accuracy, relevance and usefulness of the job description.

Grant (1989, p.5) stated that job descriptions 'are not a work schedule', however, in the past many indicated how much time is spent on different tasks. In today's work environment time percentages or frequency have been replaced with performance measures or indicators which provide a clearer indication of what is expected from the job.

Gilliland (1997, p.42) outlines the traditional components of a job description as:

- job title
- main purpose of the job
- who the individual reports to
- main tasks or areas of responsibility

For a more focused job description he suggests the following be added:

- a summary of the organisation's goals and targets
- key result areas flowing from the goals and targets
- the basic competencies needed to achieve these goals and targets
- performance criteria

Criticisms of Job Descriptions

Throughout the literature there are a number of criticisms of job descriptions. Sullivan (1996, p.1) states that there is no evidence that they 'work', may be loved by HR people, but are seldom loved by anyone else. However, many of the criticisms directed at job descriptions can be overcome if we focus on 'well written' job descriptions that meet the needs of today's work environment as the following examples show.

- 'In a fast changing environment by the time they are written they are out of date' (Sullivan, 1996, p. 1). This is the case with job descriptions that focus on duties. Job descriptions that focus on responsibilities and key result areas do not change frequently which means that they do remain current for long periods.

- 'They force individuals into job/your job conflicts and inhibits thinking outside the box creativity' (Sullivan, 1996, p. 1). Again this is true of job descriptions that look at the job in terms of duties. Job descriptions that look at the results the person is required to achieve do not prescribe what the person is required to do, they provide direction. As Plachy (1993) points out, focusing on results can encourage initiative and creativity. A quote by General George Patton illustrates this point: ' Never tell people how to do things. Tell them what to do and they will surprise you with their ingenuity' (Sacher and Sacher, 1998)
- 'They are often done by HR people who know little about the technical aspects of the job' (Sullivan, 1996, p. 1). Job descriptions for today's organisations are written by the people involved in the job such as the employee doing their job, their manager and/or members of the team that the job belongs.
- 'They can (and should) be replaced by weekly/monthly measurable (and incented) performance goals drawn up between the employee and the team' (Sullivan, 1996, p.1). It needs to be remembered that job descriptions are only one component of a human resource management system, performance measures may form part of the job description or form a separate document.

Bibliography

Albarran, Alan B. and Gregory G. Pitts: *The Radio Broadcasting Industry*, Boston, Allyn and Bacon, 2001.

Albrecht, Ulrich: *A Short Research Guide on Arms and Armed Forces*, New York, Facts on File, 1980.

Alexander, James: *Internships in Communications, Ames*, Iowa State University Press, 1995.

Allman, Paul: *Careers in Video and Digital Video*, New York: Rosen, 2001.

Anders, Peter: *Envisioning Cyberspace*, New York, McGraw-Hill, 1999.

Arkin, William M.: *Research Guide to Current Military and Strategic Affairs*, Washington, Institute for Policy Studies, 1981.

Baehr, H. and Gary A.: *Turning In On: A Reader in Women and Media*, London, Arnold, 1996.

Ball, Victoria Kloss: *Opportunities in Interior Design and Decorating Careers*, Chicago, VGM Career Horizons, 2002.

Barnouw, Erik: *A Tower in Babel: the History of Broadcasting in the United States to 1933*, New York, Oxford University Press, 1966.

Baucom, Alfred H.: *Hospitality Design for the Graying Generation: Meeting the Needs of a Growing Market*, New York, Wiley, 1996.

Baxter, John: *Australian Cinema*, Sydney, Pacific Books, 1970.

Beaman, Jim: *Interviewing for Radio*, New York, Routledge, 2000.

Berkowitz, Ira: *Vault Career Guide to Advertising*, New York, Vault, 2004.

Bertrand, Ina and Diane Collins: *Government and Film in Australia*, Sydney, Currency Press, 1981.

Bliss, Edward and James L. Hoyt: *Writing News for Broadcast*, New York, Columbia University Press, 1994.

Boella, Michael John: *Principles of Hospitality Law*, London, Cassell, 1999.

Bone, Jan, & Ana Fernandez: *Opportunities in Film Careers*, New York, VGM Career Books, 2004.

Bowers, C. A.: *The Cultural Dimension of Educational Computing: Understanding the Non-neutrality of Technology*, New York, Teachers' College Press; 1988.

Boyd, Andrew: *Broadcast Journalism: Techniques of Radio and TV News*, Woburn, Focal Press, 2001.

Brown, Douglas Robert: *The Restaurant Managers Handbook: How to Set Up, Operate, and Manage a Financially Successful Restaurant*. Lauderhill, Atlantic Pub., 1991.

Brown, James and Quaal Ward: *Radio-Television-Cable Management*, New York, McGraw Hill, 1998.

Bryant, Jennings: *Television and the American Family*, Hillsdale, Lawrence Erlbaum, 1990.

Buckingham, David: *Young People and the Media*, New York, Manchester University Press, 1993.

Buckner, Robert W.: *Site Selection: New Advancements in Methods and Technology*, New York, Lebhar-Friedman Books, 1998.

Caldwell, J. T.: *Electronic Media and Technoculture*, New Brusnwick, Rutgers University Press, 2000.

Careers in Focus: *Photography*, New York, Ferguson, 2004.

Carmouche, Rita: *Behavioural Studies in Hospitality Management*, New York, Chapman & Hall, 1995.

Carroll, Victoria: *Writing News for Television*, Ames, Iowa State University Press, 1997.

Cassiday, Doris, and Bruce Cassiday: *Careers in the Beauty Industry*, New York, Franklin Watts, 1978.

Clark, Mona: *Interpersonal Skills for Hospitality Managers*, London, Chapman Hill, 1995.

Clark, Roy Peter: *A Journalist Teaches Young Writers*, Portsmouth, Heinemann, 1987.

Cockburn, C. and Ormrod, S.: *Gender and Technology in the Making*, London, Sage, 1993.

Cohler, David Keith: *Broadcast Newswriting*, Englewood Cliffs, Prentice Hall, 1990.

Cracknell, H. L.: *Escoffier: The Complete Guide to the Art of Modern Cookery*, New York, John Wiley, 1979.

Craig, James: *Graphic Design Career Guide*, New York, Watson-Guptill, 1992.

Crawford, Tad: *Starting Your Career As a Freelance Photographer*, New York, Allworth Press, 2003.

Crouse, Chuck: *Reporting for Radio*, Chicago, Bonus Books, 1998.

Davidson, M. J. and Cooper, C. L.: *Women and Information Technology*, New York, John Wiley & Sons, 1987.

Delaney, Chuck: *Photography Your Way*, New York, Allworth Press, 2005.

Dennis, Everette E. and Edward C. Pease: *Children and the Media*, New Brunswick, Transaction Publishers, 1996.

Diamond, S. Taylor's Way: *Women, Cultures and Technology*, New York: Routledge; 1997.

Donald, Ralph and Thomas Spann: *Fundamentals of Television Production*, Ames, Iowa State University Press, 2000.

Dornenburg, Andrew: *Culinary Artistry*, New York, John Wiley & Sons, 1996.

Douglas, George H.: *The Early Days of Radio Broadcasting*, Jefferson, NC: McFarland, 1987.

Easlea, B.: *Fathering the Unthinkable: Masculinity, Scientists and the Nuclear Arms Race*, London, Pluto Press, 1982.

Ellis, Elmo: *Opportunities in Broadcasting Careers*, Chicago, VGM Career Books, 2005.

Faulkner, W. and Arnold, E.: *Smothered by Invention: Technology in Women's Lives*, London, Pluto Press, 1985.

Fensch, Thomas: *Television News Anchors*, Jefferson, McFarland, 1993.

Field, Shelly: *Career Opportunities in Advertising and Public Relations*, New York, Ferguson, 2006.

Foster, Timothy R. V.: *How to Succeed As an Independent Consultant*, London: Kogan, Page, 2002.

Fox Keller, E.: *Reflections on Gender and Science*, New Haven, Yale University Press, 1985.

Gardner, Garth: *Careers in Computer Graphics and Animation*, Fairfax, GGC, 2001.

Gibbs, Jenny: *Interior Design*, New York, H. N. Abrams, 2005.

Go, Frank M.: *Human Resource Management in the Hospitality Industry*, New York, Wiley, 1996.

Goldfarb, Roz: *Careers by Design*, New York, Allworth Press, 2001.

Gordon, Sandra R.: *Great Jobs for Film Majors*, Chicago, VGM Career Books, 2004.

Graham, Duane: *The Remarkable Story of Otto Graham*, Wayne, Immortal Investments Publishing, 2004.

Green, E. and Adam, A. Virtual Gender: *Technology, Consumption, and Identity*, New York, Routledge, 2001.

Greenman, Robert: *The Adviser's Companion*, New York, Columbia Scholastic Press Association, 1991.

Griffiths, D.: *The Exclusion of Women from Technology*, London, Pluto Press, 1985.

Hall, Ken G.: *Australian Film: the Inside Story*, Sydney, Summit Books, 1980.

Hewitt, John: *Airwords: Writing for Broadcast News, Mountain View*, Oxford, Mayfield Pub. Company, 2002.

Higham, Robin: *A Guide to the Sources of United States Military History*, Hamden, Archon Books, 1975.

Hilliard, Robert L. and Michael C. Keith: *The Broadcast Century and Beyond*, Boston: Focal Press, 2001.

Hinkin, Timothy R.: *Cases in Hospitality Management: A Critical Incident Approach*, New York, Wiley, 1995.

Holloway, J. C. : *Towards a Core Curriculum for Tourism: A Discussion Paper*, London, The National Liaison Group for Higher Education in Tourism, 1995.

Horstede, G.: *Cultures and Organizations: Software of the Mind*, London, McGraw-Hill Book Company, 1991.

Hungerland, Buff: *Marketing Your Creative Portfolio*, Upper Saddle River, Prentice Hall, 2003

Jain, S. C.: *Women and Technology*, Jaipur, Rawat Publications, 1985.

Jefferson, Michael: *Breaking into Graphic Design*, New York, Allworth Press, 2005.

Jensen, Clayne R.: *Opportunities in Recreation and Leisure Careers*, Lincolnwood, VGM Career Horizons, 2000.

Jones, Sue Jenklyn: *Fashion Design*, New York, Watson-Guptill, 2002.

Kieffer, John: *The Photographer's Assistant*, New York, Allworth, 2001.

Kirkham, P.: *The Gendered Object*, Manchester, Manchester University Press, 1996.

Kissane, Sharon F.: *Career Success for People with Physical Disabilities*, Lincolnwood, VGM Career Horizons, 1997.

Kring, Robin: *Party Creations: Book of Theme Event Design*, Denver, Clear Creek Pub., 1993.

Kurzweil, R.: *The Age of Spiritual Machines*, New York, Viking, 1999.

Lavery, P.: *Tourism Marketing and Management Handbook*, New York, Prentice Hall, 1989.

Lewis, Robert C.: *Cases in Hospitality Marketing and Management*, New York, John Wiley, 1997.

MacCloskey, Monro: *How to Qualify for the Service Academies*, New York, Richards Rosen Press, 1964.

Maclay, Edgar Stanton: *A History of the United States Navy 1771-1893*, New York, Appleton Co., 1894.

Mauro, Lucia: *Careers for Fashion Plates and Other Trendsetters*, Chicago, VGM Career Horizons, 2003.

McGuire-Lytle, Erin: *Careers in Graphic Arts and Computer Graphics*, New York, Rosen, 1999.

Miller, Samuel D.: *An Aerospace Bibliography*, Washington. Office of Air Force History, 1978.

Mitchell, Leslie Scott: *Freelancing for Television and Radio*, London; Routledge, 2005.

Mogel, Leonard: *Creating Your Career in Communications and Entertainment*, Sewickley, GATF Press, 1998.

Noronha, Shonan F. R.: *Opportunities in Television and Video Careers*, Chicago: VGM Career Books, 2003.

Orlik, Peter B.: *Career Perspectives in Electronic Media*, Ames, Blackwell Pub., 2004.

Packard, Sidney: *The Fashion Business: Dynamics and Careers*, New York, Holt, Rinehart, and Winston, 1983.

Parks, Peggy J.: *The News Media*, San Diego, Lucent Books, 2002.

Paullin, C.O.: *The Navy of the American Revolution*, Cleveland, The Burrows Brothers Co., 1906.

Perna, Rita: *Fashion Forecasting*, New York, Fairchild Publications, 1987.

Rachlis, Eugene: *The Story of the U.S. Coast Guard*, New York, Random House, 1961.

Reis, Ronald A.: *Careers in Art and Graphic Design*, Hauppage, Barrons, 2001.

Rocha, Tony L.: *Careers in Magazine Publishing*, New York, Rosen, 2001.

Rubinstein, Donna: *The Modeling Life*, New York, Berkeley Publishing Group, 1998.

Satterthwaite, Frank: *The Career Portfolio Workbook*, New York, McGraw-Hill, 2003.

Seguin, James: *Media Career Guide*, Boston, St. Martin's, 2006.

Sones, Melissa: *Getting into Fashion: A Career Guide*, New York, Ballantine, 1984.

Vogt, Peter: *Career Opportunities in the Fashion Industry*, New York, Facts on File, 2002.

Wilson, Wayne: *Careers in Publishing and Communications*, Bear, Mitchell Lane, 2002.

Yager, Fred, & Jan Yager: *Career Opportunities in the Film Industry*, New York, Ferguson, 2003.

Zahler, Karen Gantz.: *Superchefs: Signature Recipes From America's New Royalty*, New York, John Wiley & Sons, 1996.

Index

A

B

C

D

E

❑❑❑